The History of
Banbury Spencer Football Club

Brian Little

&

David Shadbolt

Published by
Robert Boyd Publications
260 Colwell Drive
Witney, Oxon OX28 5LW

Copyright © Brian Little and
David Shadbolt

First published 2013

ISBN: 978 1 908738 09 7

Printed and bound by
Berforts Information Press
Southfield Road
Eynsham, Oxford OX29 4JB

Contents

Acknowledgements

The authors would like to thank the following for the help in the production of this book, Peter Hicks, Rob Lowe, Geoff Lines and Pete Svenson.

We are also grateful for those who have given permission for material and pictures to be published. These include the Banbury Guardian, Mirror Pics, Four Shires Magazine and Banbury United Football Club.

A number of the illustrations and images published in this book are from an archive collection held by Banbury United Football Club. Unfortunately due to age and a lack of detailed records, the club no longer has any idea on the source of the material, whether there is any copyright held or whether in fact the club has the copyright. Should anyone feel that they have not been given due acknowledgment for any image or photo then the authors would be delighted to hear from them via the publishers so that this may be rectified in any subsequent reprinting.

Preface

In her sociological study of Banbury called "Tradition and Change" Margaret Stacey remarks that "there is no sport for which one club represents the town". Her unwillingness to include a particular soccer side stems from its sponsorship by a large firm which linked town and company and came up with the name Banbury Spencer Football Club.

It is for just such a reason that we have decided to devote a book to recording the history of a club which despite its name owed much to professional players from elsewhere and attracted the support of many members of the local Labour Party.

With town centre space limited and as a consequence of action by the Northern Aluminium Company to acquire Southam Road land for its sports section, Banbury Spencer Football Club was forced to rely on a ground formerly used by Stones, a printing business.

In a Coronation supplement of 1937, the Banbury Advertiser began a short section on local sports clubs by stating that "the rise of Banbury Spencer FC to prominence in the football world has been phenomenal"

It is our aim to reveal how this was achieved and to commit to print the "highs and lows" of the Gay Puritans and to afford a nostalgic look back for the many people whose lives could never have been complete without pilgrimage to the Spencer Stadium.

Introduction

Spencer Sports Club F.C. was formed in 1931 and played friendly matches on a ground closely adjoining the Middleton Road. It was the brainchild of Spencer Corsets Factory in Britannia Road and represented that company's desire to make recreational facilities available to its workforce.

In the following pages we have pursued a chronological path through a pattern of leagues, an alternation of war and peace, the influences of different managers and above all the imprint of particular players as well as the effects of cup successes which injected new enthusiasm into both the team and its supporters.

This book contains pictures which should revive memories for people from both town and area. It doesn't purport to be an exhaustive study nor a complete statistical record. Such would carry ambitions too far and be much less attractive than a focus on the highlights of the years between 1931 and 1965. For the identification of these we are grateful that newspapers and private archives make it possible to re-live both magic and tragic moments which can never dim a past determination to shout with confidence "Come on you Reds".

CHAPTER 1

The Beginnings

On Thursday January 27th 1927 the Banbury Guardian newspaper included a news item that Lucas's Factory in Britannia Road had been sold to the Spencer Corset Company of America and Manchester. The key figure in the preparations for the operation of the factory was Darwin Spencer Berger who arrived in Banbury from America the following month. He and his brother George Wendell Berger represented the Berger Corporation and became joint directors of Spencer (Banbury) Limited alongside Robert and Dorothea Allen, who had previously run the Gaylord corset factory in Manchester.

Though numbers of employees were brought down to work in the factory from the Liverpool and Manchester area, there were opportunities and training available for local people and in view of the poor employment situation, the factory was welcomed in the town. It soon became clear that another aspect of company policy was to encourage social and recreational activities by employees. This included participating in tennis, table tennis and baseball matches but it was to be football that eventually captured the imagination of followers of the game.

The football club was formed in August 1931, starting off with no more

Spencer House in Banbury, also the administration offices of Banbury Spencer Football Club until 1962 when, with the factory loosening ties with the football club, they moved out to offices in the town.

pretensions than to be a recreational activity. Nearly fifteen years after the club had been formed, at the Annual General Meeting in July 1946, then club President Robert Allen gave credit for founding the club to his wife Dorothea stating "It was her idea to give the men from Liverpool and Manchester, who came to the Spencer Works at Banbury, something to do on Saturday afternoons".

The first press references to the club appeared in the local newspapers on Thursday 3rd September 1931. The Banbury Guardian reported, "A new club has been formed in connection with Spencer Corsets Ltd, with the following officers: President, Mr Robert Allen, Captain, Mr H. Manning, Treasurer, Mr B. H. S. Gell, Secretary: Mr E. Salmons. They will play on the ground in the Middleton Road which was at one time used by the Nomads. They opened their programme there on Saturday with a match against St. Johns when they were represented by:

W.K. Gregory
J. Hobbs, G.W. Carter
A. Bywater, E. Salmons, H. Manning
F.J. Varney, F.S.M. Laver, J.F. Harper, A. Hartwell, J.H. Barratt.

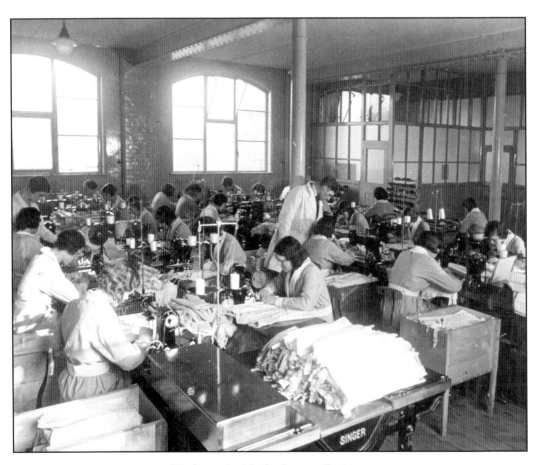

Work area inside the Spencer Factory.

The Sports Club kicked off against a stiff breeze and, though midfield play was fairly even, were in arrears at half time by 4 goals to 1. The Saints were more skilful in rounding off their attacks and in the second half doubled their interval score and won 8-2. Harper played a forceful game for the losers in his first soccer match and Hobbs and Carter were a sound pair of backs."

Whilst the first names of a number of the players who represented the club in that game have been lost over time and cannot now be traced, the following are known: William Gregory, Geoff Carter, Archie Bywater, Eddie Salmons, Hubert Manning, and Frederick, but known as Mervyn, Laver.

The Banbury Advertiser also reported the formation of the club and provided the additional information that the club would, this coming season, participate in "friendly" matches only, but hoped to prosper and in due course find their way into the local Junior League.

The club's colours were green shirts with white collars and white sleeves. However, after losing most of their early matches, in some cases by large scores, some superstitious players began to blame the green shirts so the club abandoned the green and white and opted to use the change colours of scarlet shirts with white sleeves and collars. Despite the change, results showed no significant improvement though the club did gain reputation of having good sportsmen, playing a clean game and being good losers.

The Spencer Works Canteen.

Spencer Sports Club – Early 1930s

Back Row (L to R): Cyril Brownett, J. Bolton, D. Pennock, Wally Kearse, Mervyn Laver, L.J. Stratford, K. Gregory, Eric Heavens, Archie Bywater, A. Sammons, Pennock. Middle Row (L to R): H. Elliott, C.F. Back, O. Holman, H.R. Roberts, Penrice, Percy Goodman, S. Caisbrook, Laurie Hicks, Eddie Salmons, Kendall, Joe Taylor. Front Row (L to R): H. Hands, J. Hobbs, Hubert Manning, Harry Stroud, Cyril Windrow, R.G. Tolley, H. Carter, Geoff Carter, George Sutton.   Sitting: F.J. Varney, Jack Starling

CHAPTER 2

The First Competitive Season

Undeterred by results in the club's first two seasons of friendly matches, an application was made to join the Banbury Division of the Oxfordshire Junior League for season 1933/34. Spencer were accepted and placed in Section C, the lowest level and the level at which new clubs started. When the league constitution was released in early September, the club appeared in the listings as Spencer Sports but by the time of their first fixture they had opted to be known as "Spencer Villa". The other teams in Section C were village sides Brailes, Mollington, Hornton, Shenington, Bourton, Swalcliffe and Sibford, livestock market works side Midland Marts, St Johns, Grimsbury and a side representing the 400th Battery Artillery.

Spencer's first competitive game took place at their Middleton Road ground on Saturday 23rd September 1933. Their league opponents were St Johns who took a 2-0 half time lead but Spencer, playing now in scarlet and white halves and white shorts, fought back to reduce the deficit fifteen minutes from time through J. Hobbs. Spencer then pressed for an equaliser and it came through Jack Almond. The game

Banbury Spencer 1933/34 Team Photo. Back Row (left to right): Cyril Windrow (plain clothes), H. Hands, Mervyn Laver, Penrice, Archie Bywater, F.J. Varney, Horace Williams (manager). Front Row: J Hobbs, Joe Taylor, Geoff Carter, Jack Ballinger, Hubert Manning, Eric Lowe.

finished 2-2. The Spencer Villa line up that afternoon was: Penrice (Goalkeeper), F.J. Varney (Right Back), Hubert Manning (Left Back), S. Caisbrook (Right Half), Eric Lowe (Centre Half), Mervyn Laver (Left Half), J. Hobbs (Outside Right), Joe Taylor (Inside Right), Jack Ballinger (Centre Forward), Wally Kearse (Inside Left), Jack Almond (Outside Left).

A 3-1 loss at Shenington followed before the club picked up their first ever competitive win with a 3-0 success at Sibford. A narrow 3-2 home victory over Grimsbury followed in mid October. It was at this point that the Spencer bosses showed their ambition for the club by appointing ex-professional Football League player Horace Williams to take charge of the club's playing staff.

Horace was a Welshman but it was in Scotland that he established himself in professional football, playing for St Johnstone, Hibernian and Dundee. As a centre forward he also played in the English Football League for Gillingham, New Brighton and Blackpool. Whilst at New Brighton he had earned the nickname "Hat-Trick Horace", after notching three hat-tricks in that club's first five home league fixtures of season 1926/27. Prior to coming to manage "Spencer Villa", Horace had gathered considerable coaching experience in Holland, France and Switzerland.

Horace's first game in charge saw a 5-0 home win over Sibford and the club went on to be unbeaten in their next six league games which saw Spencer move up to the top end of the table, challenging both Grimsbury and Mollington for the Championship. A home 2-1 defeat to Swalcliffe at the end of January was a set-back but the following month club officials demonstrated their ambitions to represent the town, as well as the Spencer Company, when the club's name was changed from "Spencer Villa" to "Banbury Spencer". At the same time the club announced that they intended to apply to join the Oxfordshire Senior League for the following season. Another innovation was the club issuing its first ever programme for the league game against Shenington on Saturday 24th March 1934. This was duly noted in that week's Banbury Advertiser with the newspaper reporter making the point that here was an example that the area's then more senior club Banbury Harriers, who played in the Oxfordshire Senior League, ought to seriously consider following.

Remarkably, Saturday 17th March 1934 saw the club pick up six league points. Brailes were the scheduled opposition but they were unable to raise a side so Spencer were awarded the then two points for a win. As a result of the Brailes cancellation, Spencer arranged both home and away games against the 400th Battery Artillery Club for that day. Spencer won the away game 7-0 and then the home game 9-0.

A 6-0 away win at Mollington on Good Friday 30th March, with Cyril Windrow notching four of the Spencer goals, was crucial in the club's successful quest for the Championship, as a 2-0 win at St Johns the next day meant that the title was won by a single point from both Mollington and Grimsbury.

Though Spencer were subsequently beaten 3-2 by Section "A" winners "Banbury GWR" in the divisional play-offs, it had been a most satisfactory first season of competitive football and the club was now eager to move into senior football.

During the season Spencer had started to play in scarlet rather than white shorts. A club programme at the start of the following season stated that as far as they knew they were the first club to play in "red" shorts rather than black, blue or white.

Spencer's application to join the Oxfordshire Senior League for season 1934/35 was considered at that league's annual general meeting which was held at the Oxford Town Hall on Saturday evening, 16th June 1934. Spencer had already acquired the use of the old Britannia Works football ground off Station Approach in Banbury, a ground that was to be the home of the club for the rest of its existence and is still today the home of Spencer's successor club Banbury United.

Horace Williams represented the football club at the meeting and speaking in support of the club's application said the aim was to improve the standard of football in the county and to create a larger interest in the game in Banbury by having a second Senior League side (Banbury Harriers being the then one current senior side). Horace emphasised that the club now had a very good ground and were erecting a pavilion with dressing rooms and hot and cold water.

Following a vote, Spencer were then elected to the League thus bringing to a close the club's one season of Junior League football. The full listing of teams accepted into the Oxfordshire Senior League for season 1934/35 was Banbury Spencer, Banbury Harriers, MG Sports (Abingdon), Cowley, Bicester Town,

Oxfordshire Junior League Banbury Division
Section C - Final Table 1933/4

	P	W	D	L	F	A	PTS
Banbury Spencer	22	17	3	2	79	12	37
Mollington	22	17	2	3	73	30	36
Grimsbury	22	16	4	2	54	21	36
Hornton	22	14	1	7	75	41	29
Shenington	22	10	4	8	43	44	24
Swalcliffe	22	10	2	10	57	45	22
Bourton	22	9	3	10	34	56	21
Midland Marts	22	6	2	14	50	61	14
Sibford	22	6	2	14	48	70	14
400th Battery Artillery	22	5	4	13	30	79	14
St Johns	22	4	3	15	29	79	11
Brailes	22	3	0	19	15	49	6

Chipping Norton Church Army, Headington United (the club that later become Oxford United), Heyford RAF, Pressed Steel (Cowley), Osberton Radiators (Oxford), Witney Town and Thame United.

Of little concern to Spencer at the time, the Senior League AGM had voted earlier in the evening that, in order to improve the standard of the competition, only first teams of clubs should be allowed to compete in the League, a decision which just six months later, as we shall see, had a major impact on Banbury Spencer Football Club.

Most of the players who served the club so well in that first season of competitive football had to be satisfied in subsequent seasons with reserve team football for Spencer in the Banbury Division of the Oxfordshire Junior League as players were, not surprisingly, brought into the club for the higher level of first team football. There were exceptions though.

Inside right Norman Walls and half back Eric Lowe played regularly for the club in the Oxfordshire Senior League in season 1934/35 as well as the even higher level Birmingham Combination which was to follow shortly.

Jack Ballinger, a regular in the side in 1933/34, though not going on to make first team appearances in later seasons, had a very long association with the club as he became the trainer, a role he filled for over 30 years before finally retiring after Banbury Spencer's final game in April 1965.

The most successful transition from junior to senior football though was probably that of forward Bob Kinder who moved to Banbury from Liverpool, taking up employment in the Spencer factory. He usually played either at inside left or as a left winger. He made his debut for the club in February 1934, scoring 11 league goals in the remainder of that junior league season before going on to captain the side the following season in the Oxfordshire Senior League. He remained with the club right up to the outbreak of the Second World War, adapting successfully to the higher level Birmingham Combination, turned out for Spencer during the two war time seasons in which they competed in the Oxfordshire Senior League, played in the Combination again for a couple of seasons after the War and even came out of retirement to make a

Bob Kinder

Combination appearance in April 1951! Bob made a total of 251 first team appearances in his time with Spencer, scoring 106 goals and was still involved with the club in the 1960s as he returned to Spencer in the summer of 1962 to take on a scouting role, looking for young local talent in the Banbury area.

CHAPTER 3

The Move into Senior Football

The former Britannia Works ground was much transformed after its acquisition by Spencer. The old pavilion at the ground had been demolished so a new one had to be provided for the standard of football to which Spencer were now aspiring. Two wooden railway carriages were bought and arrived at the nearby sidings. A group of volunteers assisted in manhandling these carriages and putting them into place at the ground. They were then boarded up and built around with a long covered railed veranda in front. The ground thus now had a new pavilion with ample changing room accommodation. Facilities at the ground now also included electric light, shower baths, a grandstand providing accommodation for 300 spectators, a buffet, exclusive accommodation for referees, a railed off playing area and a "double decker bus" to serve as the press box. The Banbury Guardian prior to the start of the season argued that "it is now the best appointed ground in the County, excluding the College grounds of course and not even excepting the White House Ground, the home of Oxford City."

Having been accepted into the Oxfordshire Senior League, Spencer had made an application, which was successful, to enter the FA Cup for season 1934/35. The club thus played in what was at the time the world's premier soccer cup competition, less than a year after first entering competitive football. The FA Cup draw saw Spencer given the bonus of a home game in the Extra Preliminary Round against one of the top amateur sides of that time, Hayes, who played in the Athenian League. The West London side had reached the final of the FA Amateur Cup as recently as season 1930/31 where they had lost narrowly at Highbury to Wycombe Wanderers 1-0. The game against Hayes was played on 1st September 1934, a week before the start of the club's Oxfordshire Senior League campaign, and was thus to be the club's first ever competitive fixture played at the new Spencer Stadium ground, as well as being the club's first ever game in senior football.

In preparation for senior football, Spencer adopted an "open club" policy, that is players were no longer sourced entirely from employees at the works. The club signed four players from established senior league side Banbury Harriers. These were right back Aubrey "Cobbler" Grant, goalkeeper Frank Clarke, left half Jim Hodson and right winger Arnold Mobley. Other new arrivals came down from the club's northern branches and these included inside right George Bate who had played the previous season for the Everton "A" side, inside left Ronnie Westcott a regular in the Liverpool Central League side the previous season and left full back Jim Martin previously with Lancaster Town.

The new pavilion was opened by the Mayor of Banbury, Benjamin Allsopp.

The ground was in first class condition for the Hayes game. There was practically no wind and with the sun shining it was an ideal autumn day for football. On the Spencer flags that fluttered proudly at the entrances to the ground and on the stands were the words "Welcome to Hayes". Smartly dressed boys marched around the ground selling the special "Spencer Cigarettes" and the programmes for the game. The newly built stand and then the pavilion were officially opened prior to the game by Councillor Benjamin Allsopp, the Mayor of Banbury. His speeches praised the Spencer Company for taking such interest in their employees. When opening the pavilion he said "I feel there is nothing so good as to have friendly relationships between Master and Man and nothing is better than sport and I feel confident that the employees of the Spencer Corset Company do appreciate what is being done for them. Not only for them, but also for the inhabitants of Banbury."

The sporting public of Banbury turned out in force to watch the Hayes game. The attendance was 2,874 and the Banbury Guardian reporter, in the following week's paper, claimed this showed that "there is a good local football public provided they are provided with the proper fare." They were not disappointed with what they saw either, as Banbury Spencer's performance turned out to be in excess of what surely even their most ardent supporters and the townsfolk of Banbury could have expected.

Cartoon of Banbury Spencer v Hayes game which appeared in the Banbury Guardian on Thursday 6th September 1934.

Bob Kinder won the toss for Spencer and elected for his team to defend the town goal. After 25 minutes of play, Jesse Twynham got the ball in the net for Spencer after he had received a pass from Kinder but the referee ruled he was off side. However, five minutes later Spencer were rewarded when Reg Wallis scored a fine goal. The opening of the second half saw Spencer on the offensive and after four minutes Wallis beat Wallage in the Hayes goal for the second time. Hayes then staged some promising attacks but Jim Martin, Aubrey "Cobbler" Grant and Wallis stuck to their guns well and gave nothing away with goalkeeper Frank Clarke not being seriously troubled.

Just over a quarter of an hour of the second period had ticked by when Kinder scored Spencer's third goal with the best shot of the match. Again, Hayes put on pressure, but generally the fast open tactics of the home team had them struggling and their fate was sealed seventeen minutes from the end when Wallis steered a perfect centre from Mobley into the net to complete his hat-trick. It was not until seven minutes from the end that Hayes got their only goal, this being registered by Groves. Final score: Banbury Spencer 4 Hayes 1.

The Banbury Spencer line up that afternoon against Hayes was as follows: Frank Clarke; Aubrey "Cobbler" Grant and Jim Martin; Eric Lowe, Norman Walls and Jim Hodson; Arnold Mobley, George Bate, Reg Wallis, Bob Kinder and Jesse Twynham.

After the game, the Hayes team and officials were the guests of the football club at the Crown Hotel in Bridge Street for a "New Season's Inaugural Supper", which also served as a celebration of the day's events. Club President Robert Allen in his address said that the day had been a great occasion in the history of Banbury Spencer Football Club. He added that this was only their second season in competitive football and if anyone had told them last year they would be playing a team of the calibre of Hayes everybody in Banbury would have laughed at it. Spencer manager Horace Williams, when called upon, thought he could rightly claim to be the happiest man in Banbury that night. He added that he was a former professional footballer working here for the firm and looking after the football but had never in all his experience of the game worked anywhere where there had been such a wonderful team spirit and personal touch between the heads of the firm and the team, which made them a happy family. He added that the players and himself were indebted to the joint Presidents of the club Mr and Mrs Robert Allen for the enthusiasm they passed down.

Banbury Spencer Football Club

(Members Oxon Senior League and Oxon Junior League)

NEW SEASON'S
INAUGURAL SUPPER

WELCOME TO SEASON, 1934-35

✦   ✦   ✦

THE CROWN HOTEL, BANBURY,
September 1st, 1934

We know we cannot always win, BUT, we have the will to win, and will always play to win,

— AND —

Whether we win, draw or lose, we shall play the game for the GAME'S sake in the true sporting spirit, extending to those who vanquish us the hand of good fellowship, while openly declaring our every intention to put forth an extra effort to reverse the result at our next meeting.

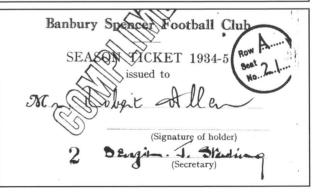

Complimentary Season Ticket for season 1934/35 issued to Club President Robert Allen.

The following week's Banbury Guardian contained a reply from Robert Allen to a letter from the Mayor of Banbury, also published in that week's paper, that wished Spencer all the best for the future and stated how impressed he had been with what he had seen at the Hayes game. Allen commented "There is no doubt what-ever that, as you say, our Club will do the town a great deal of good, inasmuch as it will bring many visitors of the sporting character, and naturally advertise Banbury as a place where one can spend a happy Saturday afternoon, and we are hopeful that the townspeople of this proud and ancient borough will rally round in support of Spencer's attempt to produce high grade soccer football in Banbury."

It had been a superb opening to Banbury Spencer's years in senior football and earned them a trip to Maidenhead United in the next round two weeks later but that turned out to be a disappointing day for Spencer as they were abruptly brought down to earth with Maidenhead romping to a 6-0 win.

Spencer's Oxfordshire Senior League campaign had begun on Saturday 8th September when a goal from Reg Wallis gave them a 1-1 draw away to Thame United. The first home Senior League game, played two weeks later, saw a 4-2 win for Spencer over Cowley with the goals coming from Bob Kinder (2), George Bate and Reg Wallis. The win over Cowley was the first in a run of five consecutive league victories to mid-December which saw Spencer in third

Oxfordshire Senior League Table as at Saturday 15th December 1934							
	P	W	D	L	F	A	PTS
Witney Town	9	7	0	2	35	15	14
RAF Heyford	7	6	1	0	36	5	13
Banbury Spencer	6	5	1	0	32	7	11
Thame United	8	4	3	1	19	13	11
Pressed Steel, Cowley	12	4	2	6	32	51	10
Chipping Norton CA	8	4	0	4	18	27	8
Bicester Town	9	4	0	5	16	14	8
MG Sports, Abingdon	9	3	2	4	19	29	8
Headington United	9	3	1	5	22	22	7
Osberton Radiators	9	3	0	6	18	33	6
Cowley	6	2	0	4	11	16	4
Banbury Harriers	10	0	2	8	17	43	2

1934/35 programme cover.

place, three points behind Witney Town and two behind RAF Heyford but with games in hand on both those clubs. This run included a 12-1 home win over Pressed Steel, Cowley and a 9-1 away win at Osberton Radiators.

The small number of Oxfordshire Senior League games played up to mid-December is explained by the club's involvement in four FA Amateur Cup games in this period. At this time football clubs were divided into professional and amateur status. Spencer were an amateur club and as such did not pay their players, other than expenses. After having been elected to senior football in the summer, the club had therefore made application to play in the national FA Amateur Cup. This had been accepted and victories over Henley Town 3-1 away, Chipping Norton Church Army 4-0 at home, Bicester Town 3-2 away and Newbury Town 3-0 away in the Qualifying Rounds earned Spencer a place in the First Round Proper (last 64), a remarkable achievement in their first season of senior football. They were drawn away to Bournemouth Gas Works Athletic, the game to be played on Saturday 12th January 1935. Though the rather unflattering club name might suggest otherwise, the Gas Works side were one of the top amateur sides of that period, having reached the FA Amateur Cup final in season 1929/30, when they lost 5-1 to Ilford at Upton Park, and been semi-finalists as recently as season 1932/33. It was thus a tough draw for Spencer but before that game there were developments which turned out to have a major impact on the future status of the football club.

On Monday December 17th 1934, Rugby Town Football Club held a meeting at which a decision was reached that, due to financial problems caused by a lack of support, they would fold and immediately tender their resignation to the Birmingham Combination. At the time, the club had just two points from 12 games and were bottom of the Combination table. The Chairman of Rugby Town attended a special meeting of the Birmingham Combination three days later and explained that the club could not continue on gates of around 300, bringing in receipts per game of just £6. Having heard of Rugby's plight and being advised that there was a possibility of another club being elected to take over their fixtures, the Spencer club saw this as an opportunity to move up to a higher level and manager Horace Williams attended the Combination meeting and offered, despite the poor record that they would be inheriting, to take over Rugby Town's fixtures. The Combination unanimously approved this and Spencer's first game was scheduled for Saturday 29th December 1934, at home to the previous season's Combination champions Dudley Town.

Spencer, having been accepted into the Birmingham Combination, then made a formal application to the Oxfordshire FA for permission to play in that competition, which they thought would be readily granted. Spencer stated that they intended to field a reserve side to fulfil their remaining Oxfordshire Senior League fixtures and would form a third team to fulfil their commitments to the Banbury Division of the Oxfordshire Junior League.

From the Banbury Guardian on Thursday January 3rd 1935.

However, on the following Thursday, Spencer received a telegram from the Oxfordshire FA stating that their application would not be considered until the next Council meeting in the New Year and that they must not play against Dudley but fulfil their Senior League fixture at home to Banbury Harriers on that date. Spencer complied with the County FA's instruction and beat their local rivals 10-2 with Reg Wallis scoring five, Jesse Twynham two and Bob Kinder, Arnold Mobley and T. Corbin getting one each.

Though the Oxfordshire FA meeting was not held until Saturday 5th January, stories appeared in Oxfordshire papers prior to the meeting that Spencer's request would be refused as the Oxfordshire FA did not want to lower the standard of the Senior League and that clubs had ruled at the previous summer's AGM that no reserve sides should be admitted to the League. This was indeed the formal outcome of the meeting and the Oxfordshire FA issued the following basic statement "The application of Banbury Spencer FC to play its Second team instead of its First team

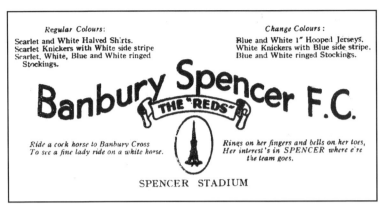

Regular Colours:
Scarlet and White Halved Shirts.
Scarlet Knickers with White side stripe
Scarlet, White, Blue and White ringed
Stockings.

Change Colours:
Blue and White 1" Hooped Jerseys.
White Knickers with Blue side stripe.
Blue and White ringed Stockings.

Banbury Spencer F.C.

THE "REDS"

Ride a cock horse to Banbury Cross
To see a fine lady ride on a white horse.

Rings on her fingers and bells on her toes,
Her interest's in SPENCER where e're
the team goes.

SPENCER STADIUM

Extract from inside a 1934/35 programme – showing the club's then nickname of the "Reds" and the famous "Ride a Cock Horse" nursery rhyme with an altered final line. From December 1934, the nickname "Reds" would disappear from the front page of the programme and be replaced by the "The Gay Puritans" logo, albeit the club was still referred to as "the Reds" inside for the rest of the season.

in the Oxon Senior League; and its Third team instead of its Second team in the Oxon Junior League should not be granted."

The Spencer Football Club Committee met the following Tuesday and decided to fulfil their Oxfordshire Senior League fixtures for the rest of the season with their first team. They issued the following statement "At the meeting of the Executive Committee of Banbury Spencer FC on Tuesday night, it was decided to take no immediate action regarding the refusal of the OFA to consider the club's application for permission to compete in the Birmingham Football Combination this season, it being quite clear from the OFA's letter dated 5th January, 1935, that the OFA will not raise any objection to the Banbury Spencer FC becoming members of the Birmingham Football Combination next season."

The next game, after confirmation that Spencer were to complete the season in the Oxfordshire Senior League, was the eagerly awaited FA Amateur Cup First Round Proper game away to Hampshire League side Bournemouth Gas Works on Saturday 12th January 1935. Spencer manager Horace Williams was particularly impressed with the ground commenting "The dressing room accommodation was as good as any First Division's side, and better than most. I should imagine it is the finest amateur ground in the country. The ground itself was very level and could be compared to a first class bowling green."

A crowd of around 3,000 turned out to see the game with home supporters expecting a relatively easy passage to the next round against this "unheard of side called Banbury Spencer".

However, it was to be far from easy for "The Lights" as the Gas Works side were known. Spencer goalkeeper Frank Clarke had an excellent first half, denying the home side with some outstanding saves though a goal from Bungay gave Bournemouth a deserved 1-0 half time lead. A reinvigorated Spencer took the game to the Gas Works at the start of the second half and equalised seven minutes after the resumption when Ronnie Westcott fastened on to a pass from Bob Kinder. It looked as though the Gas Works would be coming to the Spencer Stadium for a replay the following Saturday but with just ten minutes to go they were awarded a

The top of the front of the club programme during the second half of season 1934/35, now showing the newly adopted club nickname of the "Gay Puritans" and a quote from a poem by Richard Braithwaite, relating to his observations on Puritan zeal in Banbury from early in the 17th Century. Both the nickname and the quote would appear on all programmes for the remainder of the club's existence as Banbury Spencer.

free kick and though the resultant shot looked to be going wide, and was in any case well covered by the Spencer custodian, it then struck a home forward, the deflection giving Clarke no chance of preventing it from trickling through a pack of players and into the net. Though Spencer fought hard for an equaliser in the last ten minutes, they were unable to find one. It was a cruel blow for Spencer to lose to such a fortunate goal but the club's fine run in the FA Amateur Cup in their first season of entering the competition was over. The Spencer side that afternoon against the Gasworks was Frank Clarke; Aubrey "Cobbler" Grant, Jim Martin; Eric Lowe, Norman Walls, Jim Hodson; Reg Wallis, George Bate, Ronnie Westcott, Bob Kinder and Jesse Twynham.

After being knocked out of the FA Amateur Cup, Spencer turned their attentions back to the Oxfordshire Senior League. After the loss to the Gas Works, the club went on an unbeaten run of 11 league games, 9 wins and 2 draws, culminating in a 6-4 win over Headington United (later to become Oxford United) on Saturday 20th April 1934. The win over Headington left

Oxfordshire Senior League Final Table 1934/35							
	P	W	D	L	F	A	PTS
Banbury Spencer	22	16	3	3	90	39	35
RAF Heyford	22	14	4	4	74	29	32
Cowley	22	14	3	5	63	33	31
Witney Town	22	13	2	7	87	38	28
MG Sports (Abingdon)	22	11	3	8	56	49	25
Bicester Town	22	10	2	10	42	39	22
Headington United	22	8	2	12	49	49	18
Pressed Steel (Cowley)	22	7	4	11	59	78	18
Thame United	22	6	4	12	42	80	16
Chipping Norton Church Army	22	8	0	14	43	85	16
Osberton Radiators	22	6	1	15	44	82	13
Banbury Harriers	22	4	2	16	43	91	10

Spencer needing just one point from their final two games to secure the Championship ahead of nearest challengers RAF Heyford. However, before Spencer's penultimate league game of the season, Heyford could only manage a draw against Bicester on Monday 29th April, and so the title was won with two games to spare. Spencer were now able to concentrate on local cup competitions and fielded weakened sides in their last two Senior League games, losing both.

The season finished with Spencer drawing 2-2 on Saturday 4th May against RAF Heyford in the final of the Banbury Charity Cup at the Spencer Stadium thus sharing the cup with the airmen before, a week later, they beat Henley Town 2-0 in the final of the Oxfordshire Charity Cup, a game played at Oxford City's White House Ground. The Spencer team against Henley was Frank Clarke; Aubrey

Banbury Spencer 1934/35

Back Row (Left to Right): Eric Lowe, Aubrey "Cobbler" Grant, Norman Walls, Frank Clarke, Jim Martin, Jim Hodson, Howard Williams (manager). Front Row (Left to Right): Arnold Mobley, George Bate, Reg Wallis, Bob Kinder (captain), Jesse Twynham. Photo taken before the FA Cup game against Hayes on 1st September 1934.

"Cobbler" Grant, Jim Martin; Eric Lowe, Jim McCarthy, Jim Hodson; Oliver Twynham, Norman Walls, Ronnie Westcott, Bob Kinder and Jesse Twynham.

The club's first season of senior football had been a huge success, winning the Oxfordshire Senior League and also reaching the First Round Proper of the FA Amateur Cup. The club had scored 90 goals from just 22 league games. Reg Wallis contributed 30 of those 90 goals though the rising star of the side was undoubtedly 24 year-old centre forward Ronnie Westcott who scored 23 goals in just 15 games. Bob Kinder, who had played for the club at junior level the previous season, scored 14. It was now time for these players in particular and the club in general to test themselves at the higher level of the Birmingham Combination.

Spencer Stadium – Season 1934/35

The two railway carriages around which the pavilion was built can clearly be seen in this photo, along with the double-decker bus which served as the "Press Box".

CHAPTER 4

Into the Birmingham Combination

Banbury Spencer were formally elected as full members of the Birmingham Combination at the AGM of the League during the summer of 1935.

At this time, there were two competing semi-professional leagues in the Birmingham area. There was the Birmingham Combination, which Spencer had now joined, and also the Birmingham League. The leagues, at this point in time, were of approximately equal strength. Though most of the other sides in the Combination were semi-professional, Spencer continued to operate as an amateur club.

The full list of teams competing in the Birmingham Combination for season 1935/36 was as follows:

Aston Villa "A"	Darlaston	Redditch
Atherstone Town	Evesham Town	Shirley Town
Banbury Spencer	Gloucester City	Tamworth
Birmingham Trams	Halesowen Town	Walsall Reserves
Bournville Athletic	Hinckley United	West Bromwich Albion "A"
Bromsgrove Rovers	Leamington Town	Wolverhampton Wanderers "A"
Cheltenham Town Reserves	Market Harborough Town	

With interest in the club growing, the summer of 1935 saw the formation of a Banbury Spencer F.C. Supporters Club. Alderman Theo Clark, who became mayor of Banbury in November 1935, was elected its President.

Another change during the summer was the entering of a reserve side in the newly formed "Central Amateur League". The league was intended to provide a competition for the few strictly senior amateur clubs in the Midlands. Spencer considered that this would be a good standard of football which would help with the development of young players for the Birmingham Combination. This league involved games against sides in Leicestershire, Northamptonshire, Derbyshire and Lincolnshire. The full list of teams competing in the Central Amateur League for season 1935/36 was as follows:

Banbury Spencer	Northampton Mount Pleasant	RAF Cranwell
Ibstock Penistone Rovers	Northampton Nomads	RAF Upper Heyford
Leicester Nomads	North Derbyshire Ramblers	

Banbury Spencer strengthened their side for the Birmingham Combination by bringing to the club experienced inside right Johnnie "Jock" Wilson, who had previously played for Edinburgh City, and also signed Bicester Town goalkeeper Tommy Bott but otherwise gave the players who had done so well in the Oxfordshire Senior League the season before the opportunity to stake a claim for a place in the team at the higher level. Wilson was appointed the club's captain for the start of the season.

Spencer's debut in the Birmingham Combination was a home game against Aston Villa "A". This game was played on Saturday 31st August 1935 and the attractive opening fixture captured the interest of the local football public with a crowd of around 3,000 making their way to the Spencer Stadium. The Football League "A" sides consisted primarily of young boys trying to establish themselves in senior football. The Villa side that day included right back James Robey, centre-half Ernie "Mush" Callaghan, left half Billy Simpson, inside right Jackie Martin and left winger Charlie Drinkwater, all of whom played in the Football League for the Birmingham based side at some point in their careers. In goal was Ron Butcher who, though never making a first team appearance for Villa, later played in the Football League for Reading.

Spencer's first game at the higher level resulted in a 3-2 win. Horace Genner put Spencer in front in the 24th minute and though Callaghan equalised from the penalty spot just two minutes later, a goal from Jesse Twynham after 31 minutes gave Spencer a 2-1 half time lead. Fifteen minutes from time, Drinkwater drew the visitors level once more but three minutes later Ronnie Westcott scored Spencer's third to make the final score 3-2. Goalkeeper Tommy Bott was though the hero of the day, pulling off some excellent saves, particularly in the first half. The match reporter in the Banbury Advertiser described Bott's performance thus "he intrigued the crowd greatly with his coolness, amounting almost to nonchalance, in making the most thrilling saves, which he was called upon to do at the rate of twice per minute during some of the more intensive of the Villa's campaigns."

The Banbury Spencer line-up versus Aston Villa "A" was Tommy Bott. Aubrey "Cobbler" Grant, Jim Martin, Bill Pearson, Jim McCarthy, Norman Walls, Jesse Twynham, Johnnie "Jock" Wilson, Horace Genner, Ronnie Westcott, Bob Kinder.

Spencer won their next two league games, away to Darlaston and at home to Bournville Athletic, and in this period got past Pressed Steel of Cowley at home in the Extra-Preliminary Round of the FA Cup and Moor Green, also at home, in the First Round of the Birmingham Senior Cup, thus making it an excellent start to the season with five wins from five games in all competitions and a maximum six points (two points for a win in those days) from the three league games played.

Spencer's next game was in the league away to Wolverhampton Wanderers "A" on Monday 16th September 1935. Playing in their scarlet and white halved shirts and scarlet shorts, very colourful for that era, the Spencer players were the butt of taunts like "Where's the carnival?" "Whose circus are you?" "Play up the

Toreadors". The club's scarlet shorts were an innovation and an original idea of Robert Allen, the club President, the argument being it made it easier to pick out one's own players during the course of play. As the Spencer club's patrons were in the clothing trade, and as such brightly coloured and unusual football shorts (or knickers as they were then known) were not available to buy, they could be made to specification in the Spencer Factory. The Spencer players would have to get used to such taunts about their colourful attire.

The match itself against Wolverhampton saw Spencer, despite a hat-trick from Ronnie Westcott, lose 4-3, unluckily according to all match reports.

However, the game was more notable for the only appearance of Spencer manager Horace Williams in a competitive game for the club. George Arlett failed to get to the ground in time for kick-off, due to being

1935/36 programme cover.

delayed by a business appointment in Derby, and so the team had to be reshuffled with Williams himself playing on the right wing. He later described this appearance as "making up the numbers" and he was certainly subject to some good natured barracking from the home supporters with shouts such as "Come on Grandad". However, Wolves supporters were soon won over with his standard of play, one commenting "He looks like their Grandad, but plays like a man of 26". The Banbury Advertiser reporter, in attendance, stated "Manager Williams was certainly the hero of the day, and his experience outweighed his lack of condition. He did not attempt what he reasonably could not expect to do, but contended himself with a cool and calculated game that sent "Jock" Wilson and Ronnie Westcott through for the first two Spencer goals. The crowd were quick to appreciate his qualities and he gained quite an affectionate place in the hearts of some of them."

Though the defeat at Wolverhampton had been unfortunate, it turned out to be the start of a poor run of results for the club. There was just one win in the next eight league games and that was a narrow 3-2 away success over league strugglers Market Harborough Town. Saturday 23rd November was notable for an embarrassing 10-1 defeat away to Birmingham League side Kidderminster Harriers in the Birmingham Senior Cup and things did not improve much the following week when Spencer lost 5-2 away to Evesham Town in a league game.

The week after the Evesham game, Spencer were at home to Walsall Reserves in a league game and the match programme announced the resignation of Horace Williams as manager of the club. Though things had not worked out as well as hoped that season, it is undeniable that Horace's experience had been of immense benefit to the fledgling Banbury Spencer team that he took control of back in 1933. He had left a permanent and positive mark on the club's history and could take credit for much of its early success.

The club struggled on with no manager and with no immediate improvement in results. There were two away defeats between Christmas and New Year and the Saturday after the New Year showed how poor the club's current form was when they lost 6-0 away to Aston Villa "A", the side they had beaten 3-2 at the Spencer Stadium on the opening day of the season. The league table after the Villa game showed that Spencer had slipped to one from bottom of the table with just three wins and two draws from 15 games played. The three wins had been the club's first three games of the season as the only subsequent league win, at Market Harborough in November, was wiped out when the Leicestershire side withdrew from the Combination.

Birmingham Combination Table 1935/36 as at Saturday 4th January 1936					
	P	W	D	L	PTS
Aston Villa "A"	19	15	1	3	31
Wolves "A"	21	12	4	5	28
WBA "A"	19	13	0	6	26
Cheltenham Town Res	19	10	3	6	23
Tamworth	17	11	0	6	22
Walsall Reserves	19	10	2	7	22
Gloucester City	16	9	3	4	21
Birmingham Trams	18	7	5	6	19
Halesowen Town	17	9	0	8	18
Darlaston	17	7	3	7	17
Shirley Town	17	6	2	9	14
Hinckley United	15	5	3	7	13
Bromsgrove Rovers	15	4	4	7	12
Redditch	17	4	4	9	12
Leamington Town	13	4	3	6	11
Atherstone Town	17	4	2	11	10
Evesham Town	17	4	2	11	10
Banbury Spencer	15	3	2	10	8
Bournville Athletic	16	2	3	11	7

Towards the end of January, the club announced that they had arranged for Jimmy "Punch" McEwen to be brought into the club on a temporary basis from the coaching staff at Arsenal Football Club to train and coach the players. "Punch" had previously had a successful playing career around the turn of the century with Football League sides Luton Town, Glossop North End and Bury, including captaining the last named when they won the FA Cup in 1903 beating Derby County 6-0 at the old Crystal Palace ground. "Punch" got his first taste of football management at then Southern League Norwich City in the summer of 1907, being their player/manager for one season. He later had a spell as a scout with Fulham before, in 1914, he joined Arsenal's coaching staff, working under manager George Morrell. After Morrell's resignation in 1915, McEwen took charge of first-team affairs at the club during the remainder of World War I, becoming in effect the caretaker manager of the team that played during the War years in the London Combination. After the war had ended he was replaced by Leslie Knighton for the start of the 1919–20 season, but McEwen continued to stay with the club, working as a dressing-room attendant and as a coach under Herbert Chapman and then George Allison.

The first league game after McEwen's involvement saw Spencer beat

Birmingham Trams 4-2 away on 25th of January 1936 to register their first league victory since the middle of September, excluding the expunged Market Harborough game.

The win over the Trams began a massive upturn in fortunes, for which "Punch" can take much credit, as Spencer won 13 of their last 20 league games. This run included some impressive performances such as a 7-1 home win over Bromsgrove Rovers, a 6-3 home win and a 7-2 away win over fourth place finishers Gloucester City, and a 3-0 home win over fifth place finishers Tamworth. The improved form saw Spencer finish the season in 9th place out of 19 teams.

The club's season finished with an appearance in the final of the Oxford-shire Senior Cup. This brought the club into conflict with the Oxfordshire FA for the second time in just 18 months. The date of the final, against Oxfordshire Senior League runners up Headington United (later Oxford United), was set for Easter Monday 13th April, a date on which Spencer were due to entertain Redditch United in a Birmingham Combination game. Spencer, apparently concerned about the problems and costs of postponing the Redditch

Birmingham Combination Final Table 1935/36						
	P	W	D	L	F	A	PTS
Aston Villa "A"	36	25	3	8	126	54	53
WBA "A"	36	25	3	8	119	71	53
Wolves "A"	36	23	4	9	99	58	50
Gloucester City	36	21	6	9	99	62	48
Tamworth	36	22	2	12	118	65	46
Walsall Reserves	36	21	3	12	98	57	45
Cheltenham Town Res	36	19	6	11	79	61	44
Darlaston	36	16	8	12	86	70	40
Banbury Spencer	36	16	5	15	88	90	37
Birmingham Trams	36	13	9	14	66	64	35
Shirley Town	36	14	4	18	86	94	32
Halesowen Town	36	14	3	19	88	115	31
Evesham Town	36	13	5	18	73	107	31
Leamington Town	36	12	6	18	65	84	30
Atherstone Town	36	10	7	19	82	93	27
Bromsgrove Rovers	36	9	7	20	65	100	25
Redditch	36	8	8	20	66	108	24
Hinckley United	36	9	5	22	60	133	23
Bournville Athletic	36	2	6	28	50	127	10

fixture, wrote to the County FA stating that they wished to withdraw from the Senior Cup competition. The letter read "Herewith we make formal application to withdraw from the final of the Oxon Senior Cup, thereby giving our opponents the game. We trust that you will let us have a favourable reply."

Needless to say, and probably not a total surprise to the club, the Oxfordshire FA replied in the negative and Spencer were obliged to meet their Senior Cup commitments and postpone the Redditch game. The final was played at Oxford City's White House Ground on Easter Monday 13th April, the two sides drawing 1-1 in front of a huge crowd of 5,638. The replay on Saturday 2nd May, again at Oxford City in front of a crowd of over 5,000, was won by Headington 1-0, Spencer sending a reserve side on the same day to Halesowen Town to complete their Combination fixtures. Remarkably the reserves won 1-0.

Fitting Oxfordshire Senior Cup fixtures into the schedule would though no longer be a problem for Spencer after this season as the Oxfordshire FA, at that summer's AGM, gave the club permission to enter their reserve side into the competition, a concession that had already been granted to Oxford City who competed in the Isthmian League.

The club's reserve side finished in sixth place out of eight teams in the Central Amateur League but this was to be the only season that Spencer played in this competition. It was stated at the club's AGM in July 1936 that the reason for withdrawing from the league was the excessive travelling costs which the club could no longer afford to bear. In addition, they hoped that by entering a reserve side in the Oxford-

Programme advert for Spencer branded cigarettes available at the Spencer Stadium.

shire Senior League, the League now being willing to accept Spencer's reserves having refused to do so just 18 months earlier when the club initially wanted to join the Combination, the visit of more local sides would attract larger crowds to the Spencer Stadium for reserve team games, also helping the club's finances.

Amongst the players who made their debuts for Spencer in that first season of Birmingham Combination football, probably the most significant was an 18 year-old forward named Dick Pike.

Dick was educated in Shoreham and had made a name for himself playing for the Sussex schoolboys and youth sides. He had played for Shoreham Town and was also an amateur on the books of Arsenal Football Club when he signed for Banbury Spencer early in November 1935. As with many of the Banbury Spencer players of the time, Dick took up employment with Spencer Corsets in the town, working in the offices. He was a replacement in the Spencer side for centre forward Ronnie Westcott who had just left Spencer after signing on professional terms for the Arsenal. His first game for Banbury Spencer was on Saturday 9th November 1935 in a home Birmingham Combination game against Hinckley United when he scored one of the Banbury goals in a 3-3 draw.

Dick Pike

Dick went on to score 39 goals for Spencer from just 32 appearances in season 1935/36.

Dick continued to play for Spencer until his goalscoring exploits earned him a move to then Football League Division One side West Bromwich Albion in March 1938. He made his first team debut for Albion on Good Friday April 7th 1939 but this turned out to be Dick's only Football League appearance as his football career was disrupted by the Second World War which broke out just months later. After the War, Dick returned to Banbury Spencer and played for the club in seasons 1945/46 to 1948/49 inclusive. Dick holds the distinction of scoring more goals for the club in its 34 year history than any other player, 218 in all competitions.

Season	Total App	League App	Cup App	Total Goals	League Goals	Cup Goals
1935/36	32	27	5	39	35	4
1936/37	45	37	8	54	40	14
1937/38	31	30	1	44	44	0
1945/46	8	7	1	4	4	0
1946/47	39	34	5	39	35	4
1947/48	34	25	9	38	21	17
1948/49	2	2	0	0	0	0
Total	**191**	**162**	**29**	**218**	**179**	**39**

Dick Pike's Banbury Spencer career appearances and goals.

CHAPTER 5

The Arsenal Connection

The early days of Banbury Spencer Football Club saw them develop an unofficial relationship with Arsenal Football Club. Margate Football Club were Arsenal's recognised professional nursery club but there is much evidence to suggest that the famous London club considered Spencer as an unofficial amateur nursery with some of the Arsenal's young, still amateur, players being "loaned" to Spencer to develop their careers and any talent unearthed by Spencer being closely monitored and then given the opportunity to play and impress for the junior Arsenal sides.

The first suggestion of a relationship between the clubs came to light in September 1934. After beating Hayes in the First Qualifying Round of the FA Cup, Spencer travelled to play Maidenhead United in the Second Qualifying Round on Saturday 15th September 1934. Prior to the Maidenhead game a telegram was received by the club from George Allison, the Arsenal manager, which read "Congratulations on your splendid record. Carry on the good work. Our eyes are on our Banbury babes."

Whilst there was some secrecy over the relationship in its early days and also how it had come about, George Allison, in an address to Spencer supporters in September 1936, referred to club President Robert Allen as one of Arsenal's most enthusiastic supporters. Spencer's manager from October 1933 to December 1935, Horace Williams, also had Arsenal connections which had begun in the days when the London club were managed by Herbert Chapman. Williams, when discussing the tie-up between the clubs early in season 1935/36, acknowledged the considerable help that Chapman had given him when he was coaching the Lucerne Club in Switzerland.

The inter-change of players between the clubs began in the summer of 1935 when Spencer centre-forward Ronnie Westcott and centre-half Jim McCarthy both signed amateur forms for Arsenal, though Spencer confirmed both would continue to play for the club, at least for the immediate future. Although McCarthy never went on to play professionally for Arsenal, Westcott subsequently did so.

Then in early October 1935, Spencer used the Arsenal connection to sign two players who were on amateur terms with the North London club. These were inside left Wilf Walsh and winger Mal Griffiths. Both went on to play professionally for the Gunners.

Meanwhile, Ronnie Westcott's form in the first few months of season 1935/36 had been attracting a lot of interest from professional clubs. Sheffield United scouts were at the Atherstone Town v Banbury Spencer Birmingham Senior Cup game on Saturday 26th October 1935 and, though there primarily to watch an Atherstone player, were so impressed with Westcott that they sent the following letter to the Spencer Club, believing him to be a professional player:

> Dear Sir,
>
> We have recently had good reports from our representative regarding your centre-forward, Westcott, and it is our intention to be present at your match on Saturday next, the 2nd November, at Market Harborough. In the meantime I shall be glad to learn from you the lowest price which you would be prepared to accept for the player's transfer. A reply by return of post will be esteemed.
>
> Yours faithfully J.E. Davison
> Secretary-Manager

Westcott though never played at Market Harborough as Spencer allowed him to play for the Arsenal Combination side on that Saturday. He did turn out for Spencer the following Tuesday, in a home Birmingham Senior Cup replay against Atherstone. That game saw Arsenal manager, George Allison, at the Spencer Stadium and the next day Westcott signed professional forms for the London club thus ending his 14 month spell with Spencer.

With Westcott having left permanently for Arsenal, Spencer replaced him with another player on Arsenal's books as an amateur, Dick Pike. Though never going on to play for Arsenal, Dick later played as a professional for West Bromwich Albion.*

The visit of George Allison to the Spencer Stadium, for the Atherstone game, and the subsequent signing by the Gunners of Westcott, gained Spencer some national newspaper publicity. Allison was a regular columnist for the Sunday Express at this time and in part of his piece for the newspaper on Sunday 10th November 1935 he praised the efficiency and organisation of the Spencer club.

Horace Williams, commenting on the Sunday Express article, stated that it had been a proud moment for him when he read Allison's remarks about the club. He also recounted that just a few days previously he had reason to visit Arsenal with one of Spencer's injured players for treatment. Whilst in Allison's office an old gentleman, Sir Frederick Wall, entered the room and in introducing Williams to him, Allison said "Sir Frederick, this is Mr Horace Williams, the manager of one of the most enterprising clubs in the country."

 At this point in time, Spencer did come out into the open as to their relationship with Arsenal as in the programme for the game against Hinckley United on

---

* Dick Pike's football career was looked at in detail in Chapter 4.

Saturday 9th November they openly and proudly acknowledged that they were a nursery to the London club, referring in evidence to the transfer of Westcott and the signings for Spencer of Wilf Walsh, Dick Pike and Mal Griffiths all of whom were amateurs on Arsenal's books. A quote from manager Williams also appeared in the following week's Banbury Advertiser "We of Banbury Spencer are proud to be recognised as the amateur nursery of the North London club."

Allison, when visiting the Spencer Stadium for the Atherstone game, had also been impressed with Spencer's scarlet shorts, or knickers as they were then known. It was reported in the following week's Banbury Advertiser that Arsenal had borrowed a set for their friendly game against Racing Club de Paris in the French capital on Monday, 11th November 1935. However, it appears to be a myth, perpetuated at the Spencer club down the years, that they actually used them as Pathe newsreel of the game clearly show Arsenal in their usual white shorts!

Another tangible outcome of the connection between the clubs occurred in the second half of season 1935/36. After Horace Williams had resigned as manager of the club in December 1935, arrangements were made the following month for Arsenal coach Jimmy "Punch" McEwan to come to the club on a temporary basis to train and coach the players.* Spencer goalkeeper Tommy Bott also signed amateur forms for Arsenal in January 1936, though he did not go on to play professionally for the club.

The Arsenal manager made another visit to the Spencer Stadium on Tuesday 15th September 1936 to see Spencer play Aston Villa "A" in a Combination game. Prior to the match, Allison was interviewed by a reporter from the Banbury Advertiser and said "We regard Banbury Spencer, although there is no direct connection between the clubs, as an annexe of the Arsenal, and a very desirable annexe too." After the game, Allison was the guest of the Supporters Club at the Crown Hotel in Bridge Street. He said, when addressing the supporters, "It is not the first time I have been here as I came to watch one of your games last season and I'm afraid I made myself very unpopular by taking one of your best players, Ronnie Westcott. Tonight, I saw your team again, and making every possible allowance, I want to say in all sincerity, you have in those boys a team of which you can be justifiably proud."

Despite the statement made by Allison to the press that evening, it appears that the relationship between the two clubs diminished quite quickly. There is no evidence of any further players moving from Spencer to Arsenal or vice-versa.

There were thus three players who played for Banbury Spencer and later played in the Football League for Arsenal. These were Mal Griffiths, Ronnie Westcott and Wilf Walsh. The remainder of this chapter looks at the football careers of these three graduates from Spencer to the lofty heights of the Arsenal.

---

* This has been discussed in detail in the previous chapter.

Mal Griffiths

Winger William Malwyn Griffiths, known as "Mal", was born in Merthyr Tydfil in 1919. He started out in local football with Merthyr Thursday before joining Arsenal Football Club, initially as an amateur, in September 1935. In October 1935, at the age of just 16 he signed for Banbury Spencer.

Mal initially played for the Spencer reserve side in the Central Amateur League and it was not until Saturday 29th February 1936 that he made his first team debut, still just 16, playing on the left wing in a 3-0 home win over Atherstone Town. His second and final first team game for the club was on the following Tuesday, again at the Spencer Stadium, but this time he was on the losing side as Banbury went down 4-3 to a West Bromwich Albion "A" side. Mal's sudden departure from the Spencer Stadium, after playing so well in those two games, was not explained at the time but years later the local press reported that it had been due to a family illness.

Mal then spent nine months on loan from Arsenal at Margate between May 1936 and February 1937. At this time he was still an amateur but on his return to Arsenal in February 1937 he turned professional.

He made his first team debut for Arsenal against Leicester City at Highbury on Saturday 2nd February 1938 going on to make 9 Football League appearances through to the end of the season scoring five goals to help Arsenal win the First Division Championship. Mal moved to Leicester City for the following season and he went on to play for them for 18 years. He made 373 Football League appearances for the Foxes scoring 66 goals and of course it would have been more except for the interruption of the Second World War. He was also in the Leicester side that lost 3-1 in the 1949 FA Cup final to Wolverhampton Wanderers with Mal scoring the goal for his side that day and in season 1953/54 he won a Second Division Championship medal with the club.

After leaving Leicester, Mal played for non-league Burton Albion. Mal also won 11 senior Welsh international caps during his career, the first against Northern Ireland in 1947 and the last against Austria in 1954. There is little argument against Mal being the player to have gone on to have the most successful professional football career after playing for Banbury Spencer.

Ronnie Westcott

Centre forward Ronnie Westcott was born in Wallasey, Merseyside in 1910 and was on Liverpool's books as a youngster. When he joined Spencer he had already gained considerable experience as an amateur, having graduated through the Birkenhead

Avenue junior team and the New Brighton Football Club reserve side to the Liverpool club.

He came to Banbury in September 1934, working in the Spencer factory, and his first appearance for the club was away to Spartan League side Maidenhead United in an FA Cup Preliminary Round game on Saturday 15th September 1934. Oddly, he made his debut at right half but from then on he usually appeared in his favoured centre forward role.

At this time Spencer were in their first season as a senior club and were playing in the Oxfordshire Senior League. This league proved to be rather easy for Ronnie as he notched up 23 league goals in 15 appearances and weighed in with another 12 goals in 15 cup games.

Ronnie signed for Arsenal on amateur terms prior to the start of season 1935/36 but with the understanding that he would carry on initially playing for Spencer and only assist Arsenal when called upon to do so. This season saw Spencer in the Birmingham Combination and, despite the higher standard of football, he took up where he had left off the previous season, scoring 17 goals in Spencer's first 14 games of the season. His last game for Spencer was on Tuesday 5th November 1935 in a Birmingham Senior Cup game at the Spencer Stadium against Atherstone Town. He left the club and signed professionally for Arsenal the day after the Atherstone game.

After initially playing in Arsenal's reserve side scoring 9 goals in 17 games, Ronnie made his first team debut for the Gunners against Wolverhampton Wanderers in a 2-2 draw at Molineux on March 28th 1936. Four days later at Highbury he scored Arsenal's goal in a 1-1 draw with Bolton Wanderers but later in the match suffered a knee ligament injury. Ronnie had an operation to try and rectify the problem but this failed to completely cure the injury and, after a specialist gave an opinion that his leg would not stand up to the strains of serious football, his football career at the age of just 25 was prematurely over.

Ronnie though at least had the distinction of wearing the famous Arsenal number 9 shirt in his two appearances for the club. His two games for Arsenal saw him play alongside such legendary names as Alex James, Eddie Hapgood, Jack Crayston and Leslie Compton.

Wilf Walsh

Wilf Walsh was born in Pontlottyn, South Wales in 1917. He was an amateur on the books of Arsenal when he signed for Banbury Spencer in October 1935. Wilf made his debut for the club away to Slough in an FA Amateur Cup game on 12th October 1935. He played at inside left and scored both the Banbury goals as Spencer lost 4-2. He went on to make 34 appearances for Spencer in season 1935/36, usually as an inside forward, scoring 13 goals. His last game for Spencer was the Oxfordshire Senior Cup Final at Oxford City's ground against Headington United on 2nd May 1936 which Spencer lost 1-0, after which he signed professionally for Arsenal. Wilf was then sent out for a couple of seasons on loan to Arsenal's official professional "nursery club" Margate and was their top goalscorer in season 1937/38 with 31 goals.

He eventually made his Football League debut at Highbury in front of a crowd of 40,296 playing at outside right against Preston North End on October 22nd 1938, a match that Arsenal won 1-0. He kept his place in the Arsenal side for the next two games, away to Bolton Wanderers and a home game against Leeds United. He did not score in those three games and these turned out to be Walsh's only three appearances for the club and he was transferred to Derby County in the summer of 1939. Wilf played, without scoring, in the Rams opening three league games of the 1939/40 season prior to the competition being cancelled due to the outbreak of War.

Wilf played for both Derby County and as a guest for Notts County in War Time football. Though he did not play for Derby in the post War regionalised competitions of season 1945/46, he was certainly with them at the start of season 1946/47 as he played in their first official post War Football League game away to Sunderland on Saturday 31st August 1946. Oddly this was his only official Football League appearance for Derby* and he eventually moved to Walsall in March 1947. Wilf made a total of 33 Football League appearances for the Saddlers and scored 4 goals before moving in July 1948 to non-league Hednesford Town. Between 1949 and 1952 Wilf returned regularly to the Spencer Stadium playing for Hednesford in Birmingham Combination games. He later had spells managing both Hednesford and Redditch.

---

* Walsh's appearances in 1939/40 were expunged from the record books due to the competition being cancelled.

CHAPTER 6

The Arrival of Jimmy Cringan

At the football club's AGM held in late July 1936, Spencer announced the appointment of Jimmy Cringan as manager of the club, albeit technically the title was player/coach as the manager's title was not officially bestowed until twelve months later.

Jimmy Cringan in his playing days at Birmingham City.

As a player Jimmy was a half back with Birmingham City making 260 Football League appearances for them between seasons 1923/24 and 1933/34 (inclusive) and in that time scoring 12 League goals. He also appeared in the 1931 FA Cup Final as part of the City side that lost 2-1 to West Bromwich Albion. Prior to being with Birmingham he had been at Sunderland and Bury though he made no first team appearances with either club. He had more recently been player/manager at Boston United for season 1934/35 and part of the following season before resigning from that post in November 1935.

As well as his managerial and coaching responsibilities, Jimmy played for Spencer regularly until the outbreak of the Second World War, after which he confined himself to managerial duties. Though normally playing in a half back role he was not averse to being up front when the need arose. His career with Spencer saw him make 80 appearances for the club, scoring 11 goals.

Jimmy remained manager until June 1961, a period in charge of 25 years, though he continued to be involved with Banbury Spencer for a further two years as the club's Secretary, a role he had combined with his football management responsibilities from the end of the Second World War.

His time in Banbury also saw him spend eight years as a Conservative member of the Banbury Town Council, losing his seat shortly before he was due to become the Town's mayor. In February 1965 he was presented with a gold watch by the Football Club and a silver rose bowl from the Supporters Club to mark the length of service that he had given to the club. He retired from the Spencer firm in October 1968 and then moved back to his native Scotland.

Cringan's first season in charge began with Spencer trouncing Bournville Athletic 6-1 at home and though the next two Combination games, at home to Cheltenham Town Reserves and Walsall Reserves, were lost, a run of nine unbeaten league games followed which gave Spencer, in early December, 17 points from 12 games. Despite the good points return, Spencer were only in mid-table at this point as their Combination schedule had been disrupted by FA Cup and FA Amateur Cup games.

Comfortable FA Cup victories over Thatcham and Pressed Steel, Cowley in the Preliminary Rounds of the competition set up a First Qualifying Round home game against established Isthmian League side Wycombe Wanderers. This was the first time that Spencer had played a side from what was considered at the time to be the top league in the country for amateur football. The reporter in the Banbury Advertiser estimated the crowd to be the largest of the season to date, around 3,000, but most spectators were to be disappointed as Spencer went behind after just five minutes and then conceded a second on 30 minutes when Jim McCarthy fisted away a goal-bound shot, only for the ensuing penalty to be converted. Wycombe

Caricature of Jimmy Cringan by Norman Edwards which appeared in the Birmingham Sports Argus during season 1951/52. (Courtesy Mirror Pics)

made it 3-0 late in the second half before Spencer grabbed an even later consolation three minutes from time when Dick Pike scored from the penalty spot after a handball offence.

The FA Amateur Cup saw Spencer beat Thatcham and then Headington United, both games at home, in the Preliminary Rounds before Cowley were beaten 3-0 at home in the First Qualifying Round. After a 4-2 win at Witney Town in the Second Qualifying Round, Spencer were drawn at home to Marlow in the Third Qualifying Round but there was to be no repeat of the club's progress to the First Round Proper of two years previously as the Spartan League side ended Spencer's run at this point with a 3-1 win.

Though Spencer had made a good start to their league campaign, the period from Saturday 19th December 1936 to Saturday 20th March 1937 saw a period of relatively mediocre results for the club. Thirteen Combination games were played in this period with the club picking up 10 points. The Combination table after a 3-2 home defeat to Birmingham Trams on 20th March showed Spencer in 10th place out of 20 clubs with 27 points from 25 games.

However, Spencer started to move up the table with three wins in four days over the Easter Weekend at the end of March, these being a 2-0 home win over Birmingham City "A" on Good Friday, a 6-1 away success at Hinckley United on Easter Saturday, with Dick Pike getting four of the goals, and then a 1-0 away win against Halesowen Town on Easter Monday.

Despite having to play twice and sometimes three times a week, the wins continued to come with seven from the nine games played in April. Such was the remarkable progress over this period that Spencer went into the last day of the season on Saturday 1st May knowing that a point at Bromsgrove Rovers would assure them of finishing as the highest placed non Football League side in the

Combination, to whom the "Tillotson Cup" (named after the League's President) was awarded on an annual basis.

A large and enthusiastic group of supporters travelled to Bromsgrove to see if Spencer could gain at least the point that they needed. Player/Coach Jimmy Cringan was missing from the team due to a head injury sustained in the Combination match against Shirley Town on the Tuesday evening. The Banbury Spencer line up against Bromsgrove was: Bill Saunders, Aubrey "Cobbler" Grant, W. Hubbard, Albert Shanks, Dai Jones, Jim McCarthy, Reg Wallis, Arnold Mobley, Dick Pike, Bob Kinder and Harry Locke.

Spencer led 1-0 at half time through a tenth minute goal from Dick Pike, a lead that was doubled four minutes into the second half when Reg Wallis headed the ball past goalkeeper Heath. Bromsgrove pulled a goal back within two minutes but shortly afterwards Wallis got his second of the afternoon to restore Spencer's two goal lead. Rovers, with twenty minutes to go, reduced the deficit to one goal once more but the win for Spencer was assured when Pike scored his second late in the half to make it 4-2.

Spencer finished third in the table, well behind both Champions Walsall Reserves and runners-up West Bromwich Albion "A" but with the next non Football League side being Tamworth down in fifth place and two points behind, the Tillotson Cup was Banbury's.

Spencer had scored 96 goals in their 38 Combination games, Dick Pike leading the way with 40 of them. There were 14 each for Reg Wallis and Bob Kinder. Pike also scored 6 in Spencer's FA Cup games and 8 in the club's FA Amateur Cup games to make it an impressive total of 54 goals in all competitions.

	P	W	D	L	F	A	PTS
WBA "A"	31	23	3	5	94	34	49
Walsall Reserves	27	21	0	6	106	39	42
Wolves "A"	32	16	7	9	83	45	39
Aston Villa "A"	31	16	4	11	71	52	36
Birmingham Trams	30	15	4	11	76	69	34
Darlaston	29	14	5	10	88	47	33
Tamworth	27	14	5	8	75	61	33
Cheltenham Town Res	26	13	6	7	59	47	32
Shirley Town	27	11	5	11	64	63	27
Banbury Spencer	25	11	5	9	63	72	27
Atherstone Town	31	11	4	16	75	103	26
Redditch	29	10	4	15	64	79	24
Gloucester City	28	10	3	15	53	58	23
Halesowen Town	25	9	5	11	49	56	23
Birmingham City "A"	30	9	5	16	58	72	23
Evesham Town	27	9	5	13	60	82	23
Hinckley United	26	10	2	14	63	85	22
Bromsgrove Rovers	26	7	6	13	38	82	20
Leamington Town	28	7	1	20	36	72	15
Bournville Athletic	31	6	3	22	52	109	15

Birmingham Combination Table 1936/37 As at Saturday 20th March 1937

Programme Cover Season 1936/37.

A notable debutant in season 1936/37 was Doug Woodward who progressed through the colts and reserve sides to make his first team debut, at the age of just 16, away to Shirley Town in a Birmingham Combination game on Saturday 13th March 1937. Playing at inside right, he scored the first of Spencer's goals that afternoon in a 2-0 win. After establishing himself in the forward line early the next season he was a regular in the side until the War forced the club to temporarily withdraw from all football at the end of season 1940/41. After hostilities had finished he returned to the Spencer Stadium but

Birmingham Combination Final Table 1936/37							
	P	W	D	L	F	A	PTS
Walsall Reserves	38	29	2	7	144	50	60
WBA "A"	38	27	5	6	110	43	59
Banbury Spencer	38	22	5	11	96	88	49
Wolves "A"	38	20	7	11	105	58	47
Tamworth	38	21	5	12	124	85	47
Cheltenham Town Res	38	18	10	10	99	63	46
Aston Villa "A"	38	20	6	12	85	55	46
Birmingham Trams	38	19	6	13	100	83	44
Darlaston	38	19	5	14	102	59	43
Shirley Town	38	17	6	15	99	83	40
Redditch	38	15	6	17	87	96	36
Gloucester City	38	13	6	19	69	81	32
Halesowen Town	38	13	5	20	69	88	31
Evesham Town	38	12	7	19	76	113	31
Atherstone Town	38	12	5	21	85	127	29
Birmingham City "A"	38	11	5	22	63	83	27
Bromsgrove Rovers	38	10	6	22	61	135	26
Hinckley United	38	10	4	24	73	146	24
Leamington Town	38	9	5	24	44	88	23
Bournville Athletic	38	8	4	26	63	130	20

after a few games up front at the start of season 1945/46, he then switched to the half back line, a position in which he predominantly played for the remainder of his football career. He became Banbury Spencer's club captain the following season and remained so until, due to chest problems, he was forced to retire from the game in October 1950. In his career with Spencer, Doug made 338 first team appearances and scored 154 goals. He later had a three year spell towards the end of the 1950s as manager of Easington Sports.

Season 1936/37 saw Bill Saunders establish himself as first choice goalkeeper for the club. Banbury born Saunders had joined local side Grimsbury in 1931, playing for them against Banbury Spencer in season 1933/34 in the Junior League. He then played for the Spencer reserve side in the early part of season 1935/36 before making his first team debut in February of that season. Season 1936/37 saw Bill kept out of the first team by Tommy Bott until late January 1937 when he took his chance and from this point on he was the Spencer first choice goalkeeper through until the end of season 1937/38. By this time Bill had played some trial games for West Bromwich Albion and he subsequently

Bill Saunders

joined them in the summer of 1938. Bill went on to play two Football League games for the Albion both in season 1938/39. The Second World War then severely interfered with Bill's football career and soon after hostilities were over he was back with Banbury Spencer, playing for the club from November 1945 to January 1951 when he had to retire from the game due to a back injury. In his career at Spencer he made 283 first team appearances.

CHAPTER 7

Seasons 1937/38 and 1938/39

Having won the Tillotson Cup, in just their second season in the Birmingham Combination, the achievement being even more noteworthy as they were one of the few amateur sides in the league, it was not surprising that the club's AGM in the summer of 1937 was very positive. Assistant Secretary George Bate, speaking in the absence of Secretary Eddie Salmons, stated in commenting upon the playing season "From the point of view of achievement we can look back upon the 1936/37 season with much satisfaction, for, in winning the Tillotson Cup we regained for Oxfordshire football some measure of its departed glory and we have set a new standard for the game in Banbury."

The AGM also saw the Treasurer, Cyril Brownett, express satisfaction at the improvement that the season had been for the club financially. He reported that though the first two season's of the club at senior level had seen losses each year of around £900, a sum equivalent today in 2013 of around £50,000, the economies instigated prior to the start of the season had restricted the loss for season 1936/37 to just £68.

Spencer club officials and supporters thus went into season 1937/38 full of optimism.

The club did not enter the FA Amateur Cup this season and after a first game exit from the FA Cup at home to Chesham United, there was nothing to distract Spencer from their Birmingham Combination fixtures. Despite this, results up to the end of October were very mediocre with Spencer picking up just 11 points from 13 games. At this point Spencer were in 8th place out of 20 teams, a rather false position as they had played more games than any other team in the Combination.

There were though a couple of impressive victories in this period, an 8-1 home win over Cheltenham Town Reserves and a 6-1 home win over Walsall Reserves, the latter game being notable for the fact that Dick Pike scored all of Spencer's six goals.

A 2-0 home win over Tamworth on Saturday 6th November 1937 was though the start of an excellent run of results as Spencer were unbeaten throughout the whole of November, December and January. A 3-0 home win over Shirley Town on Saturday 5th February extended the unbeaten sequence to 13 games with the club having picked up 23 points out of a maximum of 26. After the Shirley game, Spencer had climbed up to second place in the table with 34 points from 26 games. With Aston Villa "A" three points above Spencer and having four games in hand, there was little prospect of winning the Championship but supporters were hopeful that if the winning run could continue then retaining the Tillotson Cup was not entirely out of the question.

However, any chance that Spencer had of getting into the race for the Tillotson Cup was shattered in the next five games as the club failed to win any of them. They went on to finish the season in 7th place, twenty points behind Champions Darlaston who remarkably won every one of their last 18 league games to pip Aston Villa "A" to the Championship and also pick up the Tillotson Cup as the highest non Football League side in the table.

Officials at the club's AGM in the summer of 1938 expressed satisfaction at the season, with particular emphasis again being placed on the club's amateur status in relation to the season's league placing. It was though acknowledged that the club had lost two of their best players towards the end of the season with centre-forward Dick Pike and goalkeeper Bill Saunders both leaving to join West Bromwich Albion as professionals. However, Chairman William H. Grady assured attendees that the committee was doing everything possible to fill the gaps. Jimmy Cringan had a few words to say on what he thought

Birmingham Combination Table 1937/38 As at Saturday 5th February 1938							
	P	W	D	L	F	A	PTS
Aston Villa "A"	22	18	1	3	92	30	37
Banbury Spencer	26	15	4	7	82	41	34
WBA "A"	24	13	8	3	63	33	34
Darlaston	22	15	2	5	75	26	32
Coventry City "A"	23	13	3	7	62	37	29
Tamworth	22	13	3	6	69	46	29
Shirley Town	22	12	4	6	57	40	28
Atherstone Town	23	10	6	7	49	66	26
Walsall Reserves	21	11	3	7	61	35	25
Birmingham City "A"	23	12	1	10	56	50	25
Evesham Town	22	11	3	8	42	47	25
Birmingham Trams	24	10	3	11	33	53	23
Wolves "A"	24	10	1	13	63	47	21
Gloucester City	21	6	3	12	60	64	15
Redditch	23	7	1	15	54	79	15
Cheltenham Town Res	22	5	5	12	32	59	15
Hinckley United	23	5	3	15	38	76	13
Bromsgrove Rovers	23	4	3	16	29	84	11
Halesowen Town	22	4	2	16	37	80	10
Bournville Athletic	24	3	3	18	28	89	9

Birmingham Combination Final Table 1937/38							
	P	W	D	L	F	A	PTS
Darlaston	38	31	2	5	135	34	64
Aston Villa "A"	38	29	3	6	145	47	61
WBA "A"	38	19	13	6	96	51	51
Tamworth	38	20	8	10	119	71	48
Birmingham City "A"	38	21	5	12	86	68	47
Coventry City "A"	38	19	6	13	98	57	44
Banbury Spencer	38	19	6	13	105	68	44
Walsall Reserves	38	18	8	12	107	71	44
Evesham Town	38	18	5	15	75	89	41
Shirley Town	38	17	6	15	81	82	40
Birmingham Trams	38	17	6	15	63	79	40
Wolves "A"	38	16	7	15	101	66	39
Gloucester City	38	15	8	15	96	85	38
Atherstone Town	38	13	10	15	77	104	36
Cheltenham Town Res	38	11	11	16	67	97	33
Redditch	38	12	3	23	81	111	27
Halesowen Town	38	6	5	27	63	137	17
Bromsgrove Rovers	38	5	7	26	49	135	17
Hinckley United	38	6	3	29	49	144	15
Bournville Athletic	38	4	6	28	43	140	14

had been a good season. He said everybody should understand that it was much easier to run a professional or part professional team than an amateur team owing to employment difficulties. He acknowledged that all the players had worked hard during the season and that he appreciated their efforts to attend training though it was often very difficult for them to do so.

A notable newcomer for season 1937/38 was inside forward Tommy North who joined the club at the start of the season from Loughborough Corinthians. He went on to play in various up front positions for Spencer until the outbreak of the Second World War. During the War, Tommy played for Nottingham Forest, staying with them after the War had ended making 34 appearances, scoring 9 goals, in the still regionalised 1945/46 football programme. However, after making just one Football League appearance for Forest in season 1946/47 he returned to the Spencer Stadium for the start of season 1947/48. He left the club in November 1949, the local press confirming that Tommy's employment at Spencer's Works was being terminated and that he would therefore be signing for another football club. He later played for Rugby Town, appearing for them in their first season in the Birmingham Combination, that being season 1950/51. Tommy's brother John also played regularly for Spencer from December 1950 through to the end of season 1952/53, later returning to the Spencer Stadium part way through season 1956/57 for a final few months with the club.

The first ten weeks of the following season, 1938/39, saw Spencer predominantly occupied by FA Cup and FA Amateur Cup games, the latter competition the club once more entering after a year's absence.

It was a tough draw in the Extra Preliminary Round of the FA Cup as Spencer had to visit Isthmian League side Oxford City. However, a goal from Albert Shanks earned Spencer a 1-1 draw at the White House ground before City were beaten 2-1 in the replay at the Spencer Stadium with goals from Reg Wallis and Tommy North. Morris Motors were then beaten in the Preliminary Round and Slough in the First Qualifying Round, both away from home and both by the same scoreline of 2-0. Spencer's reward was an away game against Hayes in the Second Qualifying Round. There was though to be no repeat of Spencer's famous 4-1 win over Hayes back in 1934/35 as the West London side were comfortable winners by five goals to two.

The FA Amateur Cup campaign for 1938/39 began with Spencer beating Witney Town at home 6-0 and then Bicester Town, also at home, 3-0 in the Extra Preliminary and Preliminary Rounds. A goalless draw away to Wallingford Town in the First Qualifying Round brought the Berkshire side to Banbury for a replay and Spencer made no mistake at the second attempt winning 8-0, Tommy North getting a hat-trick with Doug Woodward and Bertie Aston both getting two and Bob Kinder one. The Second Qualifying Round saw Spencer beat Windsor & Eton at the Spencer Stadium 5-3, Woodward getting four of the goals. This brought Spencer a Third Qualifying Round game at home to Slough. Having beaten Slough away in the FA Cup just five weeks previously, hopes were high of Spencer gaining a place in the Fourth Qualifying Round, just one round before the First Round Proper. However, Slough got their revenge for their earlier FA Cup defeat that season, winning 1-0 and they went on to beat Oxford City and then Wycombe Wanderers before bowing out of the competition in the last 32 when losing 3-0 at home to St Albans City. This is the last season in which Spencer entered the FA Amateur Cup.

The number of cup games played in the first ten weeks of the season had resulted in the club getting behind with their Birmingham Combination fixtures. In fact, after losing to Slough in the FA Amateur Cup on 5th November 1938, Spencer had at that point played a total of 11 FA Cup and FA Amateur Cup games but fulfilled just four Combination fixtures. Having won only one of those four league games and lost the other three, Spencer's meagre two points saw them third from bottom of the table but only above the bottom two clubs, Bromsgrove Rovers and Nuneaton Borough, on goal average, albeit with plenty of games in hand of those clubs just above them.

Having now departed from the two cup competitions, the club could focus on the League, but there was to be no immediate significant improvement in results. The new year brought little joy to the club either as there were to be five consecutive defeats from the 27th December 1938 to 21st January 1939, the latter date seeing Spencer lose 11-2 away to a West Bromwich Albion "A" side, a

Birmingham Combination Table 1938/39 As at 5th November 1938							
	P	W	D	L	F	A	PTS
Darlaston	11	10	0	1	49	7	20
Walsall Reserves	13	9	2	2	37	14	20
Aston Villa "A"	14	6	5	3	41	18	17
Wolves "A"	13	7	3	3	24	15	17
WBA "A"	12	7	1	4	36	17	15
Birmingham City "A"	11	6	2	3	37	17	14
Cheltenham Town Res	14	7	0	7	33	49	14
Coventry City "A"	12	6	1	5	37	32	13
Tamworth	7	4	2	1	18	12	10
Redditch	11	4	2	5	24	26	10
Birmingham Transport	8	4	1	3	24	17	9
Solihull Town	9	4	1	4	20	21	9
Gloucester City	8	2	4	2	8	9	8
Hinckley United	10	3	2	5	23	28	8
Atherstone Town	10	2	2	6	19	39	6
Halesowen Town	9	2	0	7	20	33	4
Bournville Athletic	9	2	0	7	10	40	4
Banbury Spencer	4	1	0	3	4	10	2
Bromsgrove Rovers	10	1	0	9	14	41	2
Nuneaton Borough	9	1	0	8	12	45	2

Birmingham Combination Table 1938/39 As at 21st January 1939 Bottom 10							
	P	W	D	L	F	A	PTS
Tamworth	18	9	4	5	50	35	22
Birmingham Transport	17	8	3	6	43	38	19
Solihull Town	17	8	1	8	44	39	17
Hinckley United	19	6	5	8	53	51	17
Halesowen Town	18	3	4	11	35	65	10
Nuneaton Borough	20	5	0	15	27	75	10
Bromsgrove Rovers	20	3	3	14	30	66	9
Bournville Athletic	20	3	2	15	31	93	8
Banbury Spencer	15	3	1	11	23	43	7
Atherstone Town	19	2	2	15	27	105	6

record Combination defeat for the club. After the Albion game Spencer were down in 19th place out of 20 teams with just 7 points from 15 games, albeit their large number of early season cup games meant they still had games in hand.

Results did start to show some improvement from February 1939 onwards and, aided by a good finish with five wins in the last seven games, Spencer finished the season in 14th place out of 20 clubs with 30 points from 38 games though this was the lowest placing to date in the club's four year tenure in the Birmingham Combination.

The loss of centre forward Dick Pike to West Bromwich Albion towards the end of season 1937/38 had clearly been a major blow to the club. After scoring 105 league goals the previous season, the club managed only 69 in 1938/39. Doug Woodward moved to centre-forward from the inside right position that he had occupied for most of season 1937/38 and scored 23 of Spencer's 69 goals but the resultant vacant inside position proved problematical with eight different players tried in that position throughout the season.

The Annual Report at the club's AGM held in July 1939, whilst acknowledging that overall it had been a disappointing campaign, expressed the view that the improved displays towards the end of the season offered hope for a better season to come.

However, developments outside of football were soon to change all those aspirations.

Birmingham Combination Final Table 1938/39							
	P	W	D	L	F	A	PTS
Aston Villa "A"	38	26	8	4	130	38	60
Walsall Reserves	38	27	5	6	129	54	59
Birmingham City "A"	38	24	4	10	124	48	52
Darlaston	38	26	0	12	120	52	52
Tamworth	38	22	7	9	112	64	51
WBA "A"	38	22	5	11	101	52	49
Wolves "A"	38	22	4	12	101	63	48
Gloucester City	38	16	12	10	73	61	44
Coventry City "A"	38	20	3	15	112	86	43
Birmingham Transport	38	19	5	14	91	86	43
Redditch	38	14	9	15	74	74	37
Cheltenham Town Res	38	17	1	20	91	110	35
Solihull Town	38	14	4	20	68	83	32
Banbury Spencer	38	11	8	19	69	87	30
Hinckley United	38	9	10	19	77	116	28
Halesowen Town	38	8	7	23	77	137	23
Nuneaton Borough	38	9	4	25	66	127	22
Atherstone Town	38	9	2	27	74	170	20
Bromsgrove Rovers	38	6	6	26	62	129	18
Bournville Athletic	38	4	6	28	51	165	14

Banbury Hospital Fete 1939

The employees, both men and women, of the Spencer Works were very supportive of the football club at this time. This photograph shows a group of ladies, all of whom worked at Spencer's, that decided to enter a float in the 1939 Banbury Hospital Fete, electing to go as the Banbury Spencer football team. From left to right standing: Vera Taylor, Jessie Pearsall, Eleanor Anthony, Doris Fortnum, Ethel Harris, Reene Ashton and Kathleen Tooth. From left to right sitting: Ivy Lambourne, Joyce Humphries, Joan Hobbs, Iris Cross and Betty Collins. In the cab is Mrs Stutchbury, her husband was the driver

CHAPER 8

The War Years

Though War Clouds were looming menacingly over Europe, the 1939/40 season began as normal. Banbury Spencer's first game was at home to Gloucester City in the Birmingham Combination on Saturday 26th August 1939. Three second half goals, from Alby White, Tommy North and Doug Woodward, gave Spencer a 3-1 win.

The game against Gloucester was though more notable for Spencer turning out for the first time in their new colours of scarlet and gold halved shirts and scarlet shorts, having previously played in scarlet and white halves with scarlet shorts. These so called "fancy colours", an innovation for the time, caused plenty of comment from supporters of opposing sides in the coming years.

Spencer's second game of the season, on Saturday 2nd September, saw them lose 3-0 away to Hinckley United, again in the Combination, but within 24 hours War had been declared on Germany and with an immediate ban being placed by the government on the assembly of crowds, the Combination programme was duly abandoned.

A few weeks later, the government, realising that football was important to the morale of a population now at War, and in conjunction with the FA, gave permission for the organisation of competitive football matches based on local areas. At the top level of the game in England, Football League

---

Let More Colour into the Game

The issue of colour in soccer kits was to re-surface in 1950 when Jon MacAdam, a Daily Express reporter, wrote an article entitled "Let More Colour into the Game". This bemoaned the lack of variety of colours in football kits and he referred specifically to Banbury Spencer:

If you think the point is a trivial one, we do not agree, and here is no other than Jimmy Cringan, brother of Scots international Willie, himself a former Celtic, Sunderland and Birmingham City half-back, and now secretary-manager of Banbury Spencer in the Birmingham Combination, to agree with us.

Recalling our recent praise of Northampton Town's natty maroon and white, Jimmy says he is all in favour of brighter coloured shirts and shorts that would add something to the grand old game.

He has been 13 years at Banbury, "and we have experienced the advantage of bright colours. Our colours are scarlet and gold halved shirts, scarlet shorts and scarlet and gold hooped stockings. The goalkeeper is in an emerald green jersey and shorts."

There is another strip in case of a colour clash but it is difficult to imagine how the question might arise, but if it does, the side goes into green and white hoops with green shorts and the goalkeeper into gold jersey and scarlet shorts.

They're certainly colour conscious at Banbury, even to the extent of having their scarlet and blue badge emblazoned on shirt pockets and shoulder flashes. Apart from having the regulation amount of green grass, they have yellow goalposts. All of this, says Jimmy Cringan, adds up to good visibility for one and all.

clubs were split into eight geographical groups. Banbury Spencer decided to continue playing football and opted to enter a side in the Oxfordshire Senior League for season 1939/40, the League commencing in mid-October.

Spencer won their first game in the Senior League away to Pressed Steel "A" 5-3 on Saturday 14th October 1939. Whilst the standard of Spencer's team was not up to that which started the season in the Birmingham Combination, it was considerably stronger than the reserve side that would have competed in the League if hostilities had not broken out. Spencer went on to win the League with 36 points from 22 games, losing just four games and finishing four points ahead of second placed Pressed Steel "A". Doug Woodward played in all 22 games and was Spencer's leading goalscorer with 38 goals.

A notable debutant in season 1939/40 was Ernie Barnes who played at right half-back in Spencer's opening game of the season against Gloucester City. Ernie had joined the club from Banbury Harriers during the summer of 1939. He was the younger brother of Tom and George Barnes who had both played a few games for the club the previous season. Ernie went on to play for Spencer both in the first and reserve teams for many years after the end of the War, establishing himself in the full back role. He was captain of the reserve side that won the Leamington & District Championship in season 1951/52 as well as the Leamington Junior Cup and Leamington Charity Cup that season. After finishing playing, he served the club as the reserve team's trainer. His first team career at the Spencer Stadium saw him make 174 appearances for the club.

Despite the increasing demands of the armed forces on young men, Spencer announced in August 1940 that they would again enter a side in the Oxfordshire Senior League for the forthcoming season. An advert was placed in the local papers that anyone interested in playing at that level should contact the club, an appeal

Oxfordshire Senior League Table 1939/40	P	W	D	L	PTS
Banbury Spencer	22	18	0	4	36
Pressed Steel "A" (Cowley)	22	16	0	6	32
Brize Norton Services	22	13	3	6	29
Headington United	22	13	1	8	27
Bicester Town	22	13	0	9	26
Oxford City Reserves	22	11	0	11	22
Infantry Training Centre	22	8	5	9	21
Cowley	20	6	5	9	17
Morris Motors	21	6	2	13	14
Osberton Radiators	22	6	2	14	14
Thame United	22	6	1	15	13
Bicester Services	19	3	1	15	7

BANBURY SPENCER F.C.

APPLICATIONS INVITED for players 1940-41 season. all positions.
Write stating previous clubs, position, age.—Secretary, Spencer House, Banbury.

Advert that appeared in both the Banbury Guardian and Banbury Advertiser in August 1940.

Oxfordshire Senior League Table 1940/41	P	W	D	L	PTS
Harwell Services	26	21	2	3	44
Infantry Training Centre "A"	25	20	1	4	41
Abingdon Services	26	16	1	9	33
Brize Norton Services "A"	26	14	4	8	32
Osberton Radiators	25	13	4	8	30
Banbury Spencer	19	14	1	4	29
Headington United	24	12	2	10	26
Heyford Services	23	12	2	9	26
Pressed Steel (Cowley)	25	10	1	14	21
Oxford City Reserves	25	7	3	15	17
Benson Services "A"	21	4	3	14	11
Brize Norton Services "B"	24	4	3	17	11
Infantry Training Centre "B"	25	4	1	20	9
Benson Services "B"	20	2	0	18	4

that brought a number of enquiries.

The club managed to play 13 Senior League games up to the end of December, winning 9, drawing 1 and losing 3.

However, from this point on, the effects of the War began to make it a struggle for the club to raise a side and fulfil fixtures. Only six league fixtures were completed between the start of 1941 and the end of April. After beating Brize Norton Services "A" 2-0 at home on 22nd April, the club announced that it was unable to complete its remaining seven fixtures. At this point in time, Spencer were in 6th place in the table with 29 points from 19 games.

Caricature of Ernie Barnes
from Banbury Advertiser November 12th 1958.

Subsequently in the summer of 1941 the Spencer Club confirmed that due to difficulties in raising a side and the increasing problems of travelling to fulfil games that they were withdrawing from all football until the end of the War.

Roll of Honour

There were a number of former Spencer players who lost their lives on active service during the Second World War. These are known to include Eddie Salmons, Archie Bywater, Oliver Twynham and Alban Danson.

Eddie Salmons was the club's first Secretary. He also played at centre-half in Banbury Spencer's first ever game after the formation of the club back in August 1931, a friendly against St Johns. He can be seen in the photo of the early Spencer squad.* Eddie did not turnout for Spencer when they began to play competitively but continued to fulfil the role of Secretary until June 1939 when he was elected Chairman of the Club. He served in the RAF during the War but was killed on active service in May 1941. His name can be seen on the War Memorial tablet in St Mary's Church at Banbury.

Archie Bywater was another player to have appeared in Spencer's first game against St Johns in August 1931 and can also be seen in the same photo. He played for Spencer in their first season of competitive football in the Banbury Division of the Oxfordshire Junior League in 1933/34. Archie served as an aircraft wireless operator in the RAF during the War but was killed when his plane was shot down over France whilst on a bombing raid to Stuttgart in March 1943. His name also appears on the tablet in St Mary's Church at Banbury.

Oliver Twynham joined Banbury Spencer from local village side King's Sutton, starting out in the Spencer reserve side and making his debut at that level as a 16 year-old against Bodicote United on Saturday 24th November 1934. His first team debut came on Saturday 5th January 1935 away to Heyford RAF in the Oxfordshire Senior League, deputising for his elder brother, Jesse, on the left wing. After spending the next two seasons back with King's Sutton he returned to Spencer in October 1937. He made a total of 16 first team appearances in his two spells with Banbury. In the War, Oliver served as a private in the Oxford and Bucks Light Infantry but was killed in action at St Omer, France in 1940. His name can be seen on the War Memorial at King's Sutton, sited on the village green outside the Church.

Alban Danson joined Spencer prior to the start of season 1937/38. He moved to the area from Liverpool, took up employment at the Spencer Works and went on to make a total of 41 first team appearances for the club over the course of two seasons, primarily playing at centre half. He left the club in April 1939 and returned to the North West to join the Liverpool City police force. Alban served in the RAF during the War but was killed on active service in November 1944. His name can be seen on the War Memorial in the village of Upton, near Birkenhead, Cheshire.

Lest We Forget

* See Chapter One

CHAPTER 9

Football Resumes and Spencer opt for Professionalism

With the War in Europe having come to an end at the beginning of May 1945, the Birmingham Combination decided to run a league programme for season 1945/46. However, when the Combination season started, towards the end of August, the War in Japan had only been over for a matter of days so there had yet to be a mass demobilisation of the forces. The release of forces personnel back into civilian life was to be a slow process over the coming months and with so many men still in the armed services throughout season 1945/46, who could be and often were moved around the country and the world at short notice, it was a difficult task for clubs to put out sides of regular players. Spencer's view though was that, despite the difficulties, they needed to compete in the Combination this season as there was a real possibility that failure to do so would mean they would not be re-admitted twelve months later and might never thus get the opportunity to return to this level of football. The difficulties posed in getting players to fulfil fixtures is illustrated by the fact that in the last peace time season of 1938/39 Spencer used 31 different players in 38 Combination games whereas this season, 1945/46, 48 different players were used in just 32 games.

Spencer's first league game was at home to Birmingham City "A" on Saturday 25th August with the City Colts winning 4-0. The Spencer side that afternoon was: David Cross, Dai Jones, Aubrey "Cobbler" Grant, Arthur Blencowe, Raymond Jones, James Ryan, Colin Syme, Bob Christie, Doug Woodward, Ralph Horne and William Buck. The issue of turnover of players is once more

```
BANBURY SPENCER FOOTBALL CLUB.

    PROGRAMME:  PRICE ONE PENNY.
               Saturday August 25th 1945.

    It is with great pleasure we welcome all patrons
back to the Spencer Stadium, after a lapse of six years.

    Our visitors to-day are fielding a very strong team
and should give the Spencer Boys a chance to prove that
Banbury can still produce good footballers.

    Next Saturday, September 1st. we are due to play at
home to Headington in the F.A. Cup, Extra Preliminary
Round. Kick off 3.30 p.m.

    Give your support and cheer the boys on to victory.
    ━━━━━━━━
    BANBURY SPENCER v BIRMINGHAM CITY RESERVES.

TEAMS.
      Home Team Colours: Scarlet and Gold.

              Cross.
          D. Jones.    Grant.
      Blencowe.    R. Jones.  Ryan.
Syme.    Christie.  Woodward.  Horne.  Buck.

Referee: F. Poole.          Linesmen: N.F.Green.
(Stratford-on-Avon).                  G. Pankhurst.

E. Edwards.    Rowley.  Strong.  Hickins.  Faulkner.
           Lovering.  Shaw.  Hicklin.
            Jinks.  Smith.
              King.

Visitors Colours: Blue and White.
```

Banbury Spencer's first post War Programme which consisted of one sheet of paper.

highlighted by the fact that only Raymond Jones and Bob Christie played in Spencer's final league game of the season at the beginning of May 1946.

Spencer did not begin the season well for they failed to win any of their first eight league games, drawing just two of those. After losing their eighth game, 3-1 away to Kidderminster Harriers on Saturday 17th November, Spencer were bottom of the table. The FA Cup saw success in two Preliminary Rounds with an 8-1 home win over Headington United, followed by an 8-0 away success at Newbury Town. However, after a 3-0 win at Windsor & Eton in the First Qualifying Round, Spencer, despite home advantage, lost 5-2 to Corinthian League side Slough United in the Second Qualifying Round. Over the next six months there was little improvement in league form. At the end of March 1946, Spencer had won just three

Birmingham Combination Table 1945/46 as at Saturday 17th November 1945 Bottom 5 Places					
	P	W	D	L	PTS
Hednesford	12	4	1	7	9
Coventry City "A"	11	3	1	7	7
Tamworth	10	2	2	6	6
Birmingham City Transport	10	2	1	7	5
Banbury Spencer	8	0	2	6	2

Birmingham Combination Final Table 1945/46							
	P	W	D	L	F	A	PTS
Darlaston	32	22	4	6	117	62	48
Nuneaton Borough	32	19	4	9	113	58	42
Bromsgrove Rovers	32	19	4	9	103	91	42
Atherstone Town	32	18	4	10	91	64	40
Dudley Town	32	17	6	9	92	65	40
Kidderminster Harriers	32	15	6	11	75	57	36
Birmingham City "A"	32	16	4	12	83	65	36
Stourbridge	32	17	2	13	90	78	36
Coventry City "A"	32	12	5	15	73	80	29
Moor Green	32	13	3	16	85	94	29
Walsall Reserves	32	11	6	15	63	82	28
Wolves "A"	32	11	5	16	83	93	27
Banbury Spencer	32	10	7	15	56	79	27
Worcester City Reserves	32	12	1	19	76	102	25
Hednesford	32	9	6	17	65	89	24
Tamworth	32	9	5	18	76	108	23
Birmingham City Transport	32	4	4	24	43	117	12

Combination games all season. However, an excellent final few weeks to the season, 7 wins in their last 9 league games, saw Spencer climb up to finish in 13th place out of 17 teams.

Though it was a difficult season there were some notable players who made appearances for the club in 1945/46. One of these was Scottish born centre half Bob Salmond who had made 135 Football League appearances for then First Division Portsmouth before joining Chelsea early in season 1938/39. He made his debut for Spencer on Saturday 8th September 1945 in an FA Cup Preliminary Round game away to Newbury. Local papers reported at the time that his work in Kingham was of national importance and he would therefore be playing for Banbury Spencer for the foreseeable future. In the end he was with Spencer for the whole season, making 27 Birmingham Combination and 6 cup appearances for the club. In the second half of the season he was the Spencer captain. He did not play for the club the following season.

Bob Salmond

Scottish born Alan Orr played five games as a forward for Spencer this season, all of them in the last 22 days of the season. Remarkably, despite only appearing in five games, he scored 8 goals and was thus the Club's top goalscorer that season. It is assumed he was in the forces and played for the club whilst stationed in the area for previously he had been with Scottish club Third Lanark. After leaving Spencer, Alan had a spell with Renfrew FC but was soon back with Third Lanark as he played for them once again between 1947 and 1951. Football League Division Two side Nottingham Forest then signed him from the Glasgow based club in August 1951. He played primarily at wing half for Forest making a total of 46 Football League appearances over the four seasons 1951/52 to 1954/55.

Another player to make appearances for Spencer in 1945/46 and later play in the Football League was Dave Davidson. Prior to the War he had been a professional with Bradford Park Avenue though he had never made a Football League appearance for them. Davidson played for Banbury Spencer whilst stationed in the forces at Wycombe. According to newspaper reports of the time he was a nephew of then Banbury Spencer manager Jimmy Cringan. His first appearance for the club was on Saturday 12th January 1946 away to Birmingham City "A". Remarkably he played at left back, left half, inside left, left wing and at centre forward in the 15 Birmingham Combination games that he played for the club through to the end of that season. Davidson then

Dave Davidson

returned to Bradford Park Avenue in the summer of 1946 making his Football League debut for the Yorkshire club in their opening Division 2 game of the 1946/47 season, playing at left half away to Chesterfield in a 1-1 draw in front of a crowd of 14,473. He went on to make a total of 13 Football League appearances for Bradford, all at left half, before moving in January 1947 to Leyton Orient where he made 84 league appearances between seasons 1946/47 and 1949/50 inclusive. He again demonstrated his versatility at Orient because though initially signed as a wing half he switched to full back when regular back Ledger Ritson broke his leg at the start of the 1948/49 season, then when the club found themselves in need of a centre half Davidson filled that gap and later Orient decided that he could do a decent job in the attack and he was played at centre forward.

At a more local level, brothers Arthur, Charlie and Joe Houghton made first team appearances for the club. Charlie and Joe had both played for Spencer during the two "War Time" seasons but this season saw Arthur's debut. Arthur was known as "Arky" and he went on to make a total of 27 first team appearances, his last being in season 1952/53, but all three brothers were regulars in the reserve side for many seasons after the War. A fourth brother Tom also played for the reserve side in the early 1950s.

Club officials at the AGM in July 1946 expressed satisfaction at the season. Chairman J.A. Deacon said "With so many of our players in the Forces, it was always difficult to be sure of a team and on many Saturdays Jimmy Cringan had only about six players up to within an hour or two of the game. I want to pay him a big tribute for the way he carried on and the difficulties he overcame."

The big news of the meeting though was the announcement that the club would from the start of season 1946/47 play on a professional basis. This did not mean that all Spencer players would be professional but the option was now there to pay players. At this time it was commonplace, particularly at this level of the game, for clubs to have a mixture of professional and amateur players and this is indeed what would happen at Banbury. Manager Jimmy Cringan announced at the AGM that goalkeeper Bill Saunders, centre-forward Dick Pike, and centre-half Bob Salmond, who had all been professionals with other clubs prior to the War, had already signed on that basis for Spencer. A fourth professional signing announced was that of inside forward Doug McPhee, a former Falkirk player, who had helped Spencer out towards the end of the previous season whilst he had been in the Army. Salmond though subsequently opted to return to his native Scotland and did not actually play for the club in season 1946/47.

Cringan also confirmed that he was in negotiation with two former pre-War West Bromwich Albion players with Football League experience who had been at Bromsgrove Rovers the previous season. These were full back Jack Screen and inside forward George Dudley, both of whom joined Spencer for the start of the season.

Jack Screen

There was though a warning at the AGM from Joint President Robert Allen to supporters and the Banbury public that the club must now start to pay its own way, "You would be amazed at what it costs to run a football club. If we want good football in Banbury we have to be prepared to pay for it. In the past I have done what I could, but taxation is now so high that I can no longer put my hand in my pocket for everything. The time has come when I must ask you to help me give you some good football." Treasurer Eric Lowe, later in the meeting, stated that attendances during season 1945/46 had averaged 1,139 but that had not been sufficient for the club to pay its own way as it had only shown a small profit for the season due to the Joint Presidents, Mr and Mrs Allen, bearing the cost of many of the expenses. He concluded "to pay our way as a professional club we need an average gate of 2,000 at least."

The 1946/47 league season began well for Spencer as they won four of their first five games and at the end of September of 1946 were second in the table, a point behind Dudley Town who had won all their first five games. A 3-2 loss away to Headington United at the first hurdle in the FA Cup was though a disappointment. However, the promising start to the club's league programme did not continue and from the start of October 1946 through to a 4-3 defeat away to Worcester City Reserves on Saturday 18th January 1947, Spencer picked up just six points, two wins and two draws, from 12 games. Performances did though show some improvement from this point and aided by an impressive five wins and a draw from their last six Combination games, Spencer climbed the table towards the end of the season to finish in 10th place out of 19 clubs with 36 points from 36 games.

Birmingham Combination Table 1946/47 as at Saturday 28th September 1946 Top 5 Places				
	P	W	D	L	PTS
Dudley Town	5	5	0	0	10
Banbury Spencer	5	4	1	0	9
Moor Green	7	4	1	2	9
Hednesford	6	3	2	1	8
Kidderminster Harriers	6	4	0	2	8

Birmingham Combination Final Table 1946/47							
	P	W	D	L	F	A	PTS
Bromsgrove Rovers	36	23	4	9	105	57	50
Walsall Reserves	36	22	3	11	95	71	47
Darlaston	36	21	3	12	116	70	45
Nuneaton Borough	36	19	4	13	84	64	42
Atherstone Town	36	18	6	12	85	73	42
Tamworth	36	18	5	13	88	68	41
Stafford Rangers	36	18	5	13	81	70	41
Dudley Town	36	18	5	13	76	71	41
Stourbridge	36	16	7	13	72	75	39
Banbury Spencer	36	15	6	15	86	65	36
Kidderminster Harriers	36	16	4	16	104	84	36
Wolves "A"	36	16	4	16	72	67	36
Redditch	36	17	2	17	83	96	36
WBA "A"	36	14	5	17	83	90	33
Moor Green	36	13	5	18	71	108	31
Hednesford	36	12	4	20	85	103	28
Worcester City Res	36	10	4	22	68	99	24
Birmingham City Transport	36	5	8	23	51	107	18
Coventry City "A"	36	6	6	24	56	123	18

Joey Wilson, not to be confused with the Johnnie "Jock" Wilson who had played for the club prior to the War, made his debut for Banbury Spencer this season. He lived in Oxford and played in season 1945/46 for Headington United, at that time still an amateur side. He began 1946/47 with them and was part of their side that beat Spencer 3-2 in the FA Cup Preliminary Round on Saturday 21st September 1946. However, the right winger so impressed the relevant personnel at Banbury Spencer that he was promptly signed on professional terms by the club, making his debut just two weeks later. Joey stayed with Spencer until leaving in the summer of 1954 to return to Headington United but after just one season at the Manor Ground he was back at the Spencer Stadium and still playing for the club in season 1960/61, albeit his later years at the club saw him drop back from his original

Joey Wilson

wing position to the half back line. In his career at Banbury Spencer, Joey made 454 first team appearances, scoring 73 goals and his appearances total is the most by any player in the 34 year history of Banbury Spencer Football Club.

At the club's AGM in August 1947, Treasurer Eric Lowe reported that the average attendance at Combination games during season 1946/47 had been 1,596 and that gates had resulted in a welcome increase of around £600 in total income compared to the previous season though this had been more than wiped out by the £900 paid out to players now that the club had professional status. Manager Jimmy Cringan in his address to the meeting said that a gate of at least 1,800 was now necessary for Combination matches, "Unless we get this we shall have to drop the professionals" he added "and I think we all realise it is not possible to get sufficient good footballers locally to maintain the standard of the team. The club is showing initiative in getting the best possible players and it is up to the football public to give us the support to enable us to continue to provide the best type of football."

Neither Cringan nor Lowe, at this time, could have predicted the large numbers that would come through the Spencer turnstiles over the next few seasons. Clubs up and down the country experienced, at all levels of the game, a Post World War II soccer boom and Banbury Spencer was no exception.

CHAPTER 10

Spencer at Colchester United in the FA Cup First Round

Season 1947/48 began with a home Birmingham Combination game against Moor Green. The game saw the introduction of yellow goalposts at the Spencer Stadium. Jimmy Cringan's idea was that yellow might outline the target area better than white. The 2,058 spectators who turned up to see the season's opener might have been shocked to see the yellow posts but they may well have left the ground believing there was merit in Mr Cringan's idea as Spencer got the season off to the best of starts with a 9-0 victory and Doug McPhee, Tommy North and Dick Pike had no trouble finding the yellow target area as they all notched hat-tricks.

The good start to the season continued with Spencer winning their first five Combination games, the last of those being a 6-0 home victory over a West Bromwich Albion "A" side on Tuesday 9th September 1947. The months of September, October and November 1947 though were to be dominated by the FA Cup.

Spencer's FA Cup campaign for season 1947/48 began with a very difficult looking Extra-Preliminary Round game at home to Isthmian League side Oxford City on Saturday 6th September. The game attracted a large crowd to the Spencer Stadium, with 3,889 being in attendance to see Spencer convincingly win 5-0, Dick Pike getting three of the goals.

The Preliminary and First Qualifying Rounds gave Spencer relatively easier games as both were against sides that played in the Oxfordshire Senior League, the same league that Spencer's reserve side were playing in that season. Osberton Radiators were beaten 8-2 at the Spencer Stadium in the Preliminary Round and then M.P.R.D. (Metal & Produce Recovery Depot at Cowley) were beaten 3-0 away in the First Qualifying Round. Spencer were given a harder task in the Second Qualifying Round, a home game against Corinthian League side Maidenhead United, but Spencer convincingly overcame their amateur opponents 4-0.

They're Yellow

Do you dream, do you doubt? No, it's just another Banbury Spencer innovation. Mr Cringan thinking over the established fact that yellow shows up better than white – (centre lines on roads for example) – thought the goal posts might assist accuracy in shooting if painted yellow instead of the customary white. To avoid being off side he wrote to Mr S.F. Rous, Secretary of the F.A., and was assured that nothing in the rules of the game prevented the posts and cross bar being painted yellow. Seemingly, we could even paint pink elephants on them if we had any pink paint. So Banbury leads again in introducing another new idea. We are still, (so far as we know) the only club to wear shoulder flashes (Army fashion) bearing the Club's name, and the only club to play in scarlet shorts.

From the club's programme against Moor Green on Saturday 23rd August 1947

It is not known how long the experiment lasted before the return to traditional white but the club's programme cover for the following season, 1948/49, consisted of a colour drawing proudly displaying the yellow goalposts.

The Third Qualifying Round brought Spencer an awkward looking trip to another team of amateurs, Athenian League side Southall. An attendance of 5,019 saw the game which finished 2-2 at the end of 90 minutes but extra time had been agreed to be played in the event of a draw and Spencer scored two in the extra thirty minutes to Southall's one to win 4-3.

There were now thoughts of Spencer reaching the First Round Proper of the FA Cup for the first time in their history. If they were to do so though, they needed to beat Corinthian League side Grays Athletic away in the Fourth Qualifying Round. This game was played on Saturday 15th November and

among the 5,510 crowd were some few hundreds from Banbury who had travelled by private car, coach and by train. The one goal lead that Spencer held at the interval was well deserved on the run of play and came after 36 minutes. Good work by Pete Tanner and Doug McPhee saw the ball crossed into the centre where Tommy North, going to collect it, went down under a tackle. As he lay on the ground the ball went out to McPhee who fired it low into the net. During the last twenty minutes of the game, Grays threw everything into attack but Bill Saunders, in the Spencer goal, had a fine game and pulled off some excellent saves to ensure that Spencer went through to the First Round with a 1-0 win.

The First Round Proper draw was awaited with enthusiasm in the town. Spencer were though not to be rewarded with a game against a Football League club but were given an away tie against Colchester United, then one of the top sides in the Southern League, a competition, at that time, recognised as being the highest level of football below the Football League. Colchester, due to their past record in the competition, had been exempt until the Fourth Qualifying Round; at that stage they had beaten local rivals and fellow Southern Leaguer's Chelmsford City 3-1 at home.

Spencer's game at Colchester United was expected to be a relatively straightforward win for the home side. Sports Reporter J.C. Chaplin, writing in the Essex Newsman Herald newspaper on Friday 21st November, said "Colchester have again had the luck of the Cup draw. Banbury Spencer, against whom Colchester are drawn, at Layer Road, are one of the lesser-known clubs. They have fought their way right through from the preliminary rounds, and have reached the First Round Proper for the first time in their fifteen years' existence as a works club. Their players

How Spencer Reached the FA Cup First Round Proper

Round		Opposition	Result	Spencer Goalscorers
Extra Preliminary	H	Oxford City	W 5-0	Dick Pike (3), Doug McPhee, Doug Woodward (pen)
Preliminary	H	Osberton Radiators	W 8-2	Pete Tanner (3), Dick Pike (3), Harry Locke, Alby White
First Qualifying	A	MPRD*	W 3-0	Tommy North, Dick Pike (2)
Second Qualifying	H	Maidenhead United	W 4-0	Doug McPhee, Dick Pike, Tommy North, Doug Woodward (pen)
Third Qualifying	A	Southall	W 4-3	Tommy North, Harry Locke, Dick Pike, Doug McPhee
Fourth Qualifying	A	Grays Athletic	W 1-0	Doug McPhee

* Metal & Produce Recovery Depot, Cowley, Oxford

belong to an Oxfordshire firm of surgical appliance manufacturers. On the face of it, it looks as if Colchester are certain of getting into the Second Round. Banbury Spencer are members of the Birmingham Combination League. Of the six league matches they have played, they have won five and drawn the other. They have nine part-time pros. Their centre-forward has scored 20 goals in 15 matches. Jim Cringan, former Celtic and Birmingham half back, is their manager. Their total wage bill is £18 a week! The rules of the Birmingham Combination do not allow wages to exceed £2 a player each match. Colchester will have to strike their poorest form to lose this match. I expect them to win handsomely."

The game against Colchester United was played on Saturday 29th November 1947. A crowd of 8,500 were at Layer Road to see the contest, including several hundred who had made the long journey from Banbury.

Colchester had the majority of the game in the first half and it was against the run of play that Spencer went ahead after 15 minutes. The goal came when a move involving Harry Locke and Tommy North saw the latter take the ball around ex West Ham United centre half Ted Fenton to face Colchester goalkeeper Harry Wright out of his goal and North's well placed shot found the far corner of the net. A sustained period of pressure towards the end of the half finally brought Colchester a deserved equaliser three minutes from the interval when Andy Brown shot through a crowd of players with Bill Saunders in the Spencer goal unsighted. The second half was more equal but it was Colchester who got the winner nine minutes from time when after a shot had hit the post, the ball rebounded out to the side of the goal where Len Cater crossed it back into the danger area and in the ensuing scrimmage Bob Curry bundled the ball home. The Banbury Spencer team at Colchester was: Bill Saunders, Ernie Barnes, Jack Screen, Joe Hackett, Doug Woodward, Bertie Aston, Pete Tanner, Douglas McPhee, Dick Pike, Tommy North and Harry Locke.

The following comments on the match appeared in a London daily newspaper under the heading of "Gallant Banbury".

Extract from Colchester United's Player/Manager Ted Fenton's Programme Notes

Well, at last we arrive at the big day for this Club in today's match in the First Round proper of the FA Cup. The Club will be making history if they reach the Second Round, so we are all out to achieve that distinction. What better opposition can we have to dispute that honour than the colourful, in more ways than one, team from Oxfordshire, Banbury Spencer. We do, indeed, give them a hearty welcome on this their first visit to Layer Road, and I am sure that we will witness a good game played in the finest sporting way akin to the grand traditions of the game.

Ted Fenton

Image on left shows the front cover of the Colchester United v Banbury Spencer programme.

"Gallant Banbury, with only one defeat against them this season, made their exit from the FA Cup after fighting their way through to the first round for the first time in their history. Though defeated they went down with flying colours. Individually the Colchester players were superior but Banbury served up some good team work and fully extended the Southern League side. Hero of the team was Saunders, the goalkeeper, who gave a brilliant display, showing excellent anticipation and safe handling of the ball. Banbury surprised Colchester by taking the lead when North rounded Fenton to score. Colchester persistently attacked but it was not until three minutes from the interval that Brown equalised and the winning goal was scored when Curry bundled the ball into the net after a rebound."

Spencer had exited the FA Cup but the supporters who had travelled to Colchester must have been proud of their team, and felt that their journey had been worthwhile. From the club's point of view, the cheque received from Colchester United, for Spencer's share of the 8,500 gate, amounting to £253 and 10 shillings, was a welcome consolation and a useful bonus to club finances. Spencer manager Jimmy Cringan was subsequently keen to take some responsibility for the club's loss at Colchester. At the club's AGM, the following summer, he said he was convinced they went out through bad management on his part as they ought not to have travelled by road to Colchester on the Saturday morning. The players had arrived stiff and cold. In future, he added, if they had to journey over 80 miles they would travel on the Friday night.

CHAPTER 11

Close but no Cigar

After Spencer's exit from the FA Cup at Colchester United, it was now a diet of regular weekly Birmingham Combination games. Due to the cup progress, the club's league programme had got behind schedule. After beating Bedworth Town 6-1 away on Saturday 8th November 1947,

Birmingham Combination Table 1947/48 As at Saturday 8th November 1947 – Top 5							
	P	W	D	L	F	A	PTS
Atherstone Town	12	9	0	3	34	13	18
Wolves "A"	13	6	4	3	26	21	16
Darlaston	10	7	2	1	28	12	16
Nuneaton Borough	13	6	4	3	30	21	16
Banbury Spencer	8	7	1	0	33	7	15

Spencer had 15 points out of a maximum 16 but despite this impressive points return they were only in fifth place in the table, albeit with plenty of games in hand over the teams above them. With no floodlights in these days, it was not until the lighter evenings and final couple of months of the season that Spencer were able to start to catch up with fixtures, so games in hand over teams above them were a constant until the later stages of the season.

The loss to Colchester did not have an adverse effect on the club's immediate league form as all four games in December were won. A 2-0 defeat away to Darlaston on Saturday 3rd January 1948 was a set-back but Spencer immediately bounced back from that with a thumping

Birmingham Combination Table 1947/48 As at Saturday 10th January 1948 – Top 5							
	P	W	D	L	F	A	PTS
Nuneaton Borough	23	14	5	4	65	34	33
Darlaston	21	14	3	4	62	33	31
Atherstone Town	20	14	1	5	58	24	29
Bedworth Town	22	13	2	7	49	39	28
Banbury Spencer	15	12	1	2	54	16	25

7-1 win over Hednesford at the Spencer Stadium the following Saturday, Dick Pike getting a hat-trick. After the Hednesford game, Spencer were in fifth place in the table, with 25 points out of a possible 30, but with at least five games in hand on all the teams above them.

After beating Hednesford, Spencer went on to pick up 14 points from their next 10 games which, bearing in mind the games still in hand, kept them very much in touch with the leading pack. Next up was the Easter Holiday period and Spencer had three Combination games, all at home. On Good Friday, 26th March, Birmingham City Transport were beaten 2-0, this was followed by a 2-0 win over West Bromwich Albion "A" on the Saturday and then a 5-1 success against Stafford Rangers on Easter Monday. Remarkably a total of nearly 11,000 turned out to watch the three games, the attendances being 3,900, 3,200 and 3,850 respectively. The three wins moved Spencer to the top of the Combination table with 45 points from 28 games. Atherstone Town, who had played one game more, had the same number of points but an inferior goal average.

After the Easter period, it was into April and Spencer won their first four games that month before then entertaining second placed Atherstone Town on Saturday

Caricature of 1947/48 players which appeared in Birmingham Sports Argus
following Banbury Spencer's 7-1 win over Hednesford in January 1947.

17th April 1948. Spencer went into the game two points ahead of Atherstone and with a game in hand over their Warwickshire opponents.

		P	W	D	L	F	A	PTS
1.	Banbury Spencer	32	25	3	4	94	34	53
2.	Atherstone Town	33	25	1	7	93	38	51

A win for Spencer would thus take them four points clear of Atherstone and still have a game in hand. A victory for Atherstone would though revive their hopes of winning the Championship. This game captured the imagination of the local football public like no other league game in the history of Banbury Spencer Football Club. A ground record for the Spencer Stadium was set at the game of 5,818 and though this figure was subsequently bettered for an FA Cup game, it remained the largest ever crowd for a league game at the Spencer Stadium in the 34 year history of the club.

The attendance was also swelled by a large number of visiting supporters. According to newspaper reports of the time, Atherstone supporters were estimated to account for about 1/5th of the attendance, 47 buses were reported to have arrived. The interest in the game in Atherstone can also be demonstrated by a report in another local newspaper that homing pigeons, brought by an Atherstone supporter, were despatched from the ground to take home the half time score and final result!

Though Spencer had won their previous nine league games leading up to this one, they lost 1-0 to Atherstone, the goal coming midway through the first half. Despite the defeat, Spencer still held the advantage in the race for the Championship as though now level on points, they still had a game in hand over Atherstone and the slightly better goal average.

Spencer responded well to this defeat as they took maximum points from their next four league games. This was though not enough for Spencer to clinch the Championship as Atherstone won their next three games to leave the top of the table going into the last day of the season as follows:

	P	W	D	L	F	A	PTS	Goal Average
1. Banbury Spencer	37	29	3	5	105	37	61	2.84
2. Atherstone Town	37	29	1	7	106	40	59	2.65

The final day of the season, Saturday 1st May 1948, saw Spencer at home to mid-table Stourbridge whilst Atherstone Town were away to sixth in the table Darlaston. Spencer's chances of winning the Birmingham Combination Championship appeared extraordinarily good. A win (two points for a win in those days of course) or draw for Spencer would mean the Championship for them no matter what happened at Darlaston. A win for Atherstone and defeat for Spencer would bring into question the matter of goal average, though with Spencer having the better average by 0.19 of a goal going into the last set of fixtures, they could even afford to lose narrowly to Stourbridge provided Atherstone only won by a small margin at Darlaston.

There was a bumper 4,400 gate for the visit of Stourbridge. The Banbury Spencer team was: Bill Saunders, Jack Screen, Joe Greszik, Joe Hackett, Doug Woodward, Phil Zambra, Pete Tanner, Douglas McPhee, John Lawrence, Tommy North, Harry Locke.

The start to the game was sensational. Stourbridge went through from the kick-off and Philips, the Stourbridge centre-forward, scored with a low shot after just ten seconds. Spencer had the better of the play as the half wore on so it was rather against the run of play that Stourbridge scored their second when left winger Hallard headed in a corner from Wiseman. Just five minutes later Stourbridge scored again when Hallard ran in and thumped the ball into the net for his second goal of the game. After 62 minutes John Lawrence headed a fine goal for Spencer and this revitalised Spencer with belief that they could still get something out of the game. However, with Spencer now pushing forward, ten minutes from the end Wiseman made it 4-1 and a minute or so later the same player scored again to make it 5-1.

When the final whistle went at the Spencer Stadium, players, officials and supporters realised everything now depended on what the result was at Darlaston. Having lost so heavily, it was clear that Spencer would only win the Championship if Atherstone had failed to win at Darlaston. There wasn't long to wait as the news soon came through that Atherstone had won 2-0. Atherstone were therefore Champions on goal average with goals of 108 for and 40 against compared with Spencer's 106 for and 42 against.

	P	W	D	L	F	A	PTS	G Av
1. Atherstone Town	38	30	1	7	108	40	61	2.70
2. Banbury Spencer	38	29	3	6	106	42	61	2.52

Birmingham Combination Final Table 1947/48							
	P	W	D	L	F	A	PTS
Atherstone Town	38	30	1	7	108	40	61
Banbury Spencer	38	29	3	6	106	42	61
Bedworth Town	38	24	6	8	102	65	54
Tamworth	38	24	5	9	96	62	53
Bromsgrove Rovers	38	21	8	9	101	67	50
Nuneaton Borough	38	18	8	12	95	66	44
Darlaston	38	19	6	13	91	73	44
Dudley Town	38	17	8	13	69	56	42
WBA "A"	38	18	5	15	86	88	41
Stourbridge	38	16	8	14	86	66	40
Walsall Reserves	38	15	9	14	76	74	39
Wolves "A"	38	12	12	14	68	75	36
Stafford Rangers	38	14	6	18	68	88	34
Hednesford	38	14	4	20	86	97	32
Birmingham City "A"	38	8	11	19	57	79	27
Redditch	38	11	4	23	64	88	26
B'ham City Transport	38	7	9	22	57	106	23
Moor Green	38	6	8	24	54	111	20
Hinckley Athletic	38	7	5	26	61	115	19
Coventry City "A"	38	3	8	27	50	123	14

To miss Championship honours by such a meagre margin and on the last day of the season was a great disappointment to the team, officials and supporters. It was certainly a disappointing finish by Spencer to what had otherwise been a really good season. Spencer did pick up the Tillotson Cup for the second time in their history though this was scant consolation for missing out on the Championship. The Tillotson Cup traditionally went to the highest finishing non league club in the Combination but, unlike the rules pre-War, if the league was now won by such a club (in this season Atherstone) then it went to the next highest. Spencer had previously won the Tillotson Cup in season 1936/37 when they had finished third in the table behind Walsall Reserves and West Bromwich Albion "A".

Phil Zambra

Left half back who joined Spencer from Kidderminster Harriers in December 1947 and played in every Combination game through to the end of the season. Phil went on to make 206 appearances for the club, his last game being in August 1953 when due to a combination of injuries and for business and travelling reasons he announced his retirement.

To have lost so heavily at home to a mid-table side on the last day of the season, thus missing out on the Championship, was a shock to supporters. Rumours soon swept through the town that certain players had been out "drinking" prior to the game on the Saturday and that this was allegedly why they had turned in sub-standard performances. Secretary/Manager Jimmy Cringan carried out an investigation which appeared to show that the rumours were entirely without foundation and he responded by having printed in the following week's Banbury Advertiser the letter below:

"To the Editor,

These rumours which are so damaging to our club and players are very numerous about the town. I have every confidence in our players and it has been a pleasure to work with them, but in all fairness to our loyal supporters, and the good name of Banbury Spencer Football Club, a special investigation has been made regarding the conduct of the players concerned namely Doug McPhee, John Lawrence and Tommy North.

The findings are as follows: Left Grimsbury 11.00 am, arrived in town 11.25 am, coffee in Apple Tree Café, departed 12.05 pm, walked to George & Dragon, McPhee and Lawrence one lemon and dash, North one ginger ale, 12.25 pm departed for lunch at Crown Hotel with other players. At 12.45 pm tea was served, departed for Stadium at 1.55 pm.

Will any person(s) who can prove these findings incorrect come forward with actual facts. Information must be given by the person(s) who witnessed other than stated above. My one aim is to convince our loyal supporters that they were not let down by misbehaviour on the part of the players in question.

J A Cringan, Secretary – Manager Banbury Spencer FC"

There had been few changes in the Spencer side from week to week during season 1947/48. Goalkeeper Bill Saunders and centre-half Doug Woodward both went through the whole of the season without missing a first team game in any competition. As well as Saunders and Woodward playing in all 38 Birmingham Combination games, full back Jack Screen played in 37 whilst inside right Doug McPhee, inside left Tommy North and winger Pete Tanner all played in 36.

Spencer had scored 106 Birmingham Combination goals during the season. Leading Combination goalscorer was Dick Pike with 21 though he was closely followed in the scoring charts by Tommy North with 20. Doug McPhee with 18, Pete Tanner with 16 and Harry Locke with 15 all made important contributions.

The club's AGM in the summer of 1948 saw Treasurer Eric Lowe report that average attendances for first team games at the Spencer Stadium had risen from the previous season's 2,038 to 3,116. The 3,116 turned out to be the club's highest average for a season in their 34 year history. It was confirmed that the club had made a profit on the season (amount not disclosed) and that this would be spent on ground improvements and new players. Manager Jimmy Cringan in his address to the meeting, referring to the forthcoming season, said "I am confident the standard of football will be as good as, if not better than, last season – and that is saying something. We've got the money and we'll

Doug Saunders

spend it to give Banbury people the best entertainment in football for 35 miles around." He went on to advise the meeting that three new professionals had been signed for the coming season. These were centre-forward Frank Treagust, outside left Doug Saunders and full back Douglas Woodman. Treagust had been a prolific goalscorer with Dudley Town during the season just ended whilst Saunders had been with West Bromwich Albion and Woodman with Bath City.

CHAPTER 12

Season 1948/49

Spencer began season 1948/49 with two away Combination games and they lost both of them, an opening day 5-3 defeat at Stafford Rangers and then a 4-1 midweek drubbing at Tamworth. Despite this 2,900 spectators turned up for Spencer's opening home Combination game of the season on Saturday 28th August 1948 against Redditch. However, the home crowd were to be disappointed as Spencer failed to win again and had to settle for a point in a 1-1 draw. By the end of September the club had just four points from six games, a very disappointing start after the form shown throughout the previous season.

Action from Spencer's first home Combination game of the 1948/49 season against Redditch. Photo shows Redditch goalkeeper about to save during one of Spencer's attacks. The crowd was 2,900.

The early rounds of the FA Cup were though successfully negotiated. A 3-1 away win at Headington United's Manor Ground in the Preliminary Round was followed by a 2-1 win at Berkhamsted Town in the First Qualifying Round. Corinthian League Uxbridge were then beaten 3-1 at the Spencer Stadium to set up a Third Qualifying Round tie at home to Isthmian League Oxford City. The game against City was played on Saturday 30th October 1948, a game that captured the interest of the local football public like no other in the history of Banbury Spencer Football Club. In glorious football weather, a ground record crowd of 7,128 came through the turnstiles, an attendance that was not exceeded in the history of the club. In part this can be explained by the running of two special trains from Oxford.

The Banbury Spencer line up against Oxford City was, Bill Saunders, Ernie Barnes, Jack Screen, Joe Hackett, Doug Woodward, Phil Zambra, Joey Wilson, Doug McPhee, Frank Treagust, Tommy North, Doug Saunders.

Birmingham Combination Final Table 1948/49							
	P	W	D	L	F	A	PTS
Bedworth Town	38	30	5	3	129	38	65
Nuneaton Borough	38	23	9	6	92	44	55
Stourbridge	38	22	9	7	104	55	53
Bromsgrove Rovers	38	23	6	9	109	57	52
Hednesford	38	21	9	8	99	64	51
Tamworth	38	19	10	9	96	57	48
Walsall Reserves	38	20	7	11	88	65	47
WBA "A"	38	16	9	13	100	84	41
Wolves "A"	38	15	11	12	73	71	41
Banbury Spencer	38	15	10	13	75	68	40
Redditch	38	13	10	15	63	88	36
Stafford Rangers	38	14	7	17	66	74	35
Bilston	38	13	7	18	62	85	33
Darlaston	38	11	8	19	66	88	30
Dudley Town	38	9	11	18	54	75	29
Hinckley Athletic	38	10	9	19	62	97	29
Atherstone Town	38	10	7	21	82	96	27
Birmingham City "A"	38	7	7	24	56	86	21
Moor Green	38	7	7	24	58	111	21
Birmingham City Transport	38	1	4	33	40	170	6
Goals For adds to one more than Goals Against but that his how the table was published by League							

Spencer got off to the best of starts when the City goalkeeper slipped as he tried to deal with a back pass and Joey Wilson nipped in to put the ball into the back of the net. City fought back though and equalised on the half hour mark. Right at the start of the second half Phil Zambra restored Spencer's lead when he scored direct from a free-kick awarded just outside the penalty area. However, two goals for City in the last fifteen minutes gave them a 3-2 win and the reward of a Fourth Qualifying Round trip to Southern League side Hereford United.

Spencer's league form for season 1948/49 improved after their FA Cup exit. From the beginning of November 1948 through to the end of March 1949, Spencer picked up 19 points from 15 games but after the poor start to the league campaign this was only enough to move the club up to mid-table.

Spencer had a hectic finish to the league season, playing 16 games in just 36 days but did well enough to finish in 10th place out of 20 teams with 40 points from 38 games played.

A factor in having so many league games to play towards the end of the season was the club's success in reaching, for the first time, the final of the Birmingham Senior Cup, all of those cup games were played on Saturdays and took priority over Combination fixtures. Spencer had reached the final as follows:

Round 1	11 Sep	Home	Boldmere St Michaels	W 6-0	Doug Saunders (3), Doug Woodward (pen), Frank Treagust (2)
Round 2	09 Oct	Home	Tamworth	W 4-2	Doug Saunders (2), Pete Tanner (2)
Q-Final	20 Nov	Away	Dudley Town	W 2-1	Harry Locke (2)
S-Final	22 Jan	Home	Redditch	D 1-1	Doug Woodward (pen)
S-Final Rep	29 Jan	Away	Redditch	W 3-2	Frank Treagust, Doug Saunders, Joey Wilson

The final against Nuneaton Borough was played at Atherstone Town's ground on Saturday 19th March 1949. The Banbury Guardian reported on the large number of supporters that travelled from Banbury as follows:

The Banbury Spencer badge as worn on the Spencer shirts in the 1940s.

"Round about midday on Saturday, the Horse Fair presented an extraordinary scene as hundreds of people gathered there to board the fleet of coaches chartered by the Supporters Club to take them to Atherstone. Nothing like it had happened before in the history of local football. And these were not all the coaches, for more parties had set off from other places and still more had gone from the villages around. How many people went from Banbury and district is difficult to say, but it is safe to put the figure at well above a thousand. The official attendance given to us was approximately 6,000. Nuneaton were well represented, it being estimated that over 2,000 had travelled by special trains and coaches."

The Banbury Spencer line up was, Bill Saunders, Jack Screen, Ernie Barnes, Joe Hackett, Doug Woodward, Phil Zambra, Joey Wilson, Doug McPhee, Frank Treagust, Tommy North, Doug Saunders.

The game was goalless at half time, though it should not have been so as Doug Saunders had a "sitter" just before the interval but shot straight at the goalkeeper. Good chances had also been missed by Nuneaton. Left winger Betts headed Nuneaton in front in the 73rd minute and then seven minutes later he scored again to make it 2-0. Spencer responded just two minutes after going two behind when Doug Saunders netted following a free-kick taken by Phil Zambra but they were unable to find an equaliser and had to settle for being runners-up.

The match reporter in the Banbury Guardian wrote "Banbury Spencer did not deserve to lose their game against Nuneaton on Saturday in the final of the Birmingham Senior Cup at Atherstone. Playing as they did would have won them nine games out of ten. They had more of the play than Nuneaton and served up the better football. Prizes in football, however, are awarded for goals, and as Nuneaton got two of these to Spencer's one, they took the cup. Apart from that, the honours of the afternoon went to the Banbury team. Although the large number of their supporters who had travelled to see them play must have been disappointed that they had been defeated they could take consolation from the way they had acquitted themselves."

Leading goalscorer for Spencer in season 1948/49 was centre-forward Frank Treagust who, having joined the club prior to the start of the season, scored 36 goals in the 34 Birmingham Combination games in which he played. Doug Saunders scored 12 but he was the only other Spencer player into double figures, Spencer's Combination goal tally for the season of 75 was some way short of the previous season's 106. Full back Jack Screen was the only player to have appeared in all 38 Combination games though centre-half Doug Woodward only missed one game and inside left Tommy North just two.

Frank Treagust

Another notable event during season 1948/49 concerned the club's reserve side. The Oxfordshire FA were at this time allowing Spencer's reserve side to compete in the Oxfordshire Senior Cup. After progressing through three rounds by beating Thame United, Bicester Town and Chipping Norton Town, Spencer met Oxford City in the final on Saturday 23rd April 1949. This was Oxford City's first team, who played in the Isthmian League, in opposition and so it was no surprise that City won the game rather comfortably 3-0.

What was remarkable though was that there was a crowd of around 5,000 at Oxford University's Rugby Club Ground on Iffley Road to see the game. The Banbury Spencer line up that afternoon was Frank Taylor, Ernie Barnes, R. Palmer, Bertie Aston, Fred Fisher, Harry Locke, Sam Weller, Alby White, Maurice Baker, George Miesowicz, Arky Houghton.

With Spencer not in the race for the Combination Championship it is no surprise that attendances, particularly in the second half of the season, did not match those of the previous year. The club's AGM in the summer of 1949 reported a loss for the year of £100, attributing this to total gates falling from 84,137 the previous season to 69,868.

At the AGM, Jimmy Cringan said the club had not been as successful as the previous season and that in his view this was mainly due to injuries and luck not running their way. On the whole though he thought it had not been a bad season and the team had certainly served up attractive football. He went on to say that he was unable to give details of any new players for the coming season, commenting "I have no new players to announce at the present time – we cannot afford the money players are asking. Not one of five players approached was willing to come to us for under £6 a match. I should like to strengthen our team but I still think our present side will hold its own in the Birmingham Combination. I know there are weaknesses and I shall get some new players if I can."

Banbury Spencer – Season 1948/49. Standing (left to right): Bertie Aston, Maurice Baker, Fred Fisher, Joe Hackett, Bill Saunders (partially hidden), Doug Woodward, Jack Screen. Kneeling (left to right): Ernie Barnes, Doug McPhee, Harry Locke, Tommy North.

Crowd at a Banbury Spencer v Oxford City game – late 1940s.

CHAPTER 13

Seasons 1949/50 to 1952/53

Spencer began season 1949/50 well, losing just one of their first eight league games, though an exit from the FA Cup at the first hurdle, losing 1-0 away to Athenian League side Hayes, was a disappointment. The 12 points that Spencer had from those opening eight games saw them leading the Combination table at the end of September.

Birmingham Combination Table 1949/50 As at Saturday 24th September 1949 Top 5							
	P	W	D	L	F	A	PTS
Banbury Spencer	8	5	2	1	9	2	12
Wolves "A"	8	4	2	2	17	11	10
Bedworth Town	5	4	1	0	15	4	9
Tamworth	6	3	3	0	12	4	9
Darlaston	6	4	1	1	16	7	9

Hopes of a challenge for the Championship were though to be effectively dashed in October as Spencer played four Combination games and lost them all. This took the club down to 5th place but having played more games than most clubs this was a false position as their then 12 points from twelve games was very much a mid-table return.

Birmingham Combination Table 1949/50 As at Saturday 28th January 1950 Top 5							
	P	W	D	L	F	A	PTS
Bedworth Town	19	15	3	1	60	17	33
Walsall Reserves	24	12	4	8	55	35	28
Banbury Spencer	22	12	3	7	36	27	27
Bromsgrove Rov'rs	17	10	6	1	41	22	26
Hinckley Athletic	20	10	4	6	33	21	24

The months of November, December and January were better for Spencer as they picked up 15 points from 10 games and at the end of this period they were third in the table, albeit not serious Championship contenders due to having played so many more games than most clubs around them. Though not able to put a good run of consistent results together over the final couple of months of the season, Spencer did enough to finish in 8th place out of 20 clubs with 43 points from 38 games.

At the club's AGM in July 1950 manager Jimmy Cringan admitted they had disappointed their supporters, particularly by not getting a single point in the month of October and that the club had paid the penalty for this through poor attendances from this point on. Treasurer Eric Lowe reported

Birmingham Combination Final Table 1949/50							
	P	W	D	L	F	A	PTS
Bedworth Town	38	28	6	4	111	43	62
Bromsgrove Rovers	38	25	9	4	98	42	59
Nuneaton Borough	38	24	9	5	92	40	57
Atherstone Town	38	24	5	9	79	51	53
Walsall Reserves	38	20	5	13	88	60	45
Hinckley Athletic	38	19	7	12	71	49	45
Tamworth	38	16	12	10	80	61	44
Banbury Spencer	38	19	5	14	63	52	43
Stourbridge	38	18	3	17	81	75	39
Dudley Town	38	16	7	15	57	72	39
Moor Green	38	13	7	18	62	73	33
Bilston	38	14	3	21	63	73	31
Hednesford	38	12	7	19	65	84	31
Stafford Rangers	38	10	11	17	53	71	31
Wolves "A"	38	11	8	19	61	68	30
Darlaston	38	12	6	20	71	93	30
Redditch	38	13	3	22	63	69	29
WBA "A"	38	7	14	17	54	62	28
Lockheed Leamingt'n	38	10	4	24	49	96	24
Bir'ham City Transp'rt	38	2	3	33	34	161	7

that home attendances had dropped to an average of 1,950, with the highest being 2,598 and the lowest 1,191. Gate receipts, which included Spencer's share of away cup games, had fallen from £3,404 to £2,354, being the primary cause of the club posting a loss for the year of £750.

Season 1950/51 saw Spencer get through two FA Cup preliminary Rounds, beating Hemel Hempstead 5-1 in a replay after drawing 1-1 down in Hertfordshire and then winning 2-1 away against Huntley and Palmers of Reading. However, after comfortably beating Bicester Town 4-0 at the Spencer Stadium in the First Qualifying Round, the club went out to Slough Town in the next round losing 5-1 away after drawing 1-1 at home. Despite playing six games, the competition proved to be expensive for the club. The following statement appeared in the programme for the Combination game against West Bromwich Albion "A" on Saturday 28th October 1950.

"Banbury Spencer's experience in the FA Challenge Cup this season proved very expensive. Altogether we played six games, two at home and four away. Being a professional club we have wages to pay, plus travelling expenses and in none of the four away games did we manage to show a profit. In one instance, when we visited Huntley & Palmer's ground, each club had to put £2 into the takings to cover travelling, referee and linesmen expenses.

Our total loss for all FA Cup games was £95 (equivalent to £2,600 in 2013). Professional clubs, like ourselves, gamble each season with finances, hoping to be lucky enough to reach the First Round Proper and so meet a League club. The question remains, - is the gamble worthwhile?"

Spencer's league campaign for season 1950/51 proved uninspiring with the club being around mid-table for the whole of the season, eventually finishing in 12th place out of 20 teams with 34 points from 38 games.

A notable friendly game did though take place during season 1950/51. We take for granted now playing midweek matches under floodlights. However, in the early 1950s this was very much uncharted territory and Banbury Spencer have their place in those pioneering days, playing Headington United (now Oxford United) under lights in a friendly at the Manor Ground during December 1950.

Headington, who had turned professional and joined the Southern League in the summer of 1949, were keen to try out floodlight football which their manager had seen abroad and initially invited Oxford City to play them in a Charity game. City turned them down and so United contacted fellow professionals Banbury Spencer who were happy to give it a go with all proceeds going to a local Hospital. Unfortunately it snowed on the day of the game, Monday 18th December 1950.

The match reporter from the Banbury Guardian wrote as follows "The staging of a floodlit match made history in Oxfordshire......
...apart from its novelty, the occasion provided a remarkably good exhibition of football in view of the conditions underfoot. It was a pity the conditions were so unfavourable after the trouble the promoters had gone to, but their task was made worthwhile, for not withstanding the

Birmingham Combination Final Table 1950/51						
	P	W	D	L	F	A	PTS
Hednesford	38	24	8	6	112	53	56
Nuneaton Borough	38	26	3	9	112	65	55
Redditch	38	20	11	7	87	43	51
Stourbridge	38	23	5	10	82	55	51
Walsall Reserves	38	18	9	11	85	55	45
Stafford Rangers	38	21	3	14	82	56	45
Bromsgrove Rovers	38	16	9	13	76	66	41
Bedworth Town	38	18	4	16	59	77	40
Lockheed Leamington	38	17	2	19	65	67	36
Tamworth	38	16	3	19	92	98	35
Sutton Town	38	13	9	16	51	78	35
Banbury Spencer	38	13	8	17	64	75	34
Atherstone Town	38	12	9	17	83	81	33
Hinckley Athletic	38	14	5	19	64	74	33
Darlaston	38	14	5	19	67	80	33
Rugby Town	38	12	8	18	57	87	32
Dudley Town	38	11	7	20	59	68	29
Moor Green	38	9	11	18	61	92	29
Bilston	38	12	5	21	60	96	29
WBA "A"	38	6	6	26	39	91	18

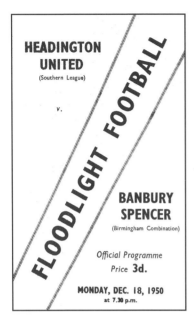

HEADINGTON
UNITED
(Southern League)

v.

BANBURY
SPENCER
(Birmingham Combination)

FLOODLIGHT FOOTBALL

Official Programme
Price **3d.**

MONDAY, DEC. 18, 1950
at 7.30 p.m.

This evening, football history will be made in Oxfordshire when the two elevens, representative of Headington United and Banbury Spencer, take the field for a friendly match in aid of the children's Christmas welfare at the Wingfield-Morris Orthopaedic Hospital, as it will be the first-ever match under artificial light in the county. We extend not only cordial greetings to Banbury Spencer but also our thanks for the noble way they slipped into the breach when a previous invitation was declined. There will be added interest in the recent announcement by the F.A. that at the next Council meeting a motion will be tabled rescinding the restriction on floodlit football, making it possible for competitive games besides those in aid of charity to be played. Progressive thought favours the availability of artificial light to assist the completion of matches during the dead winter months when darkness descends early in the afternoon.

Programme cover for the floodlight friendly (left) and extract from notes within the programme.

wintry weather which had prevailed throughout the day a crowd of over 2,600 turned up to see the game. The floodlighting was achieved by means of a dozen or so electric lamps on high poles either side of the pitch and another immediately behind each goal. From our point of view we found it fairly easy to follow the play in a general sense though it was difficult to distinguish individual players at a distance. As regards the lighting, players afterwards said it was not too bad at all – except in the middle of the field. The referee Mr Fred Williams of Oxford said he found his task a fairly hard one as he had to keep within ten yards of the ball at all times."

Headington won the game 3-0. The Spencer team was: Frank McCormack, Ernie Barnes, Joe Greszik, Bertie Aston, H. Treble (guest player from Kidlington), Ernest Ryman, Joey Wilson, Ralph Martin, Doug McPhee, Dicky Meadows, and Bernard Brock.

Banbury Spencer officials reflected on the future of floodlit football in an article in their programme for the Birmingham Combination game against Tamworth on Saturday 23rd December 1950, commenting on the floodlit game as follows "The game was for Charity, in aid of Childrens' Xmas Welfare at Wingfield-Morris Orthopaedic Hospital. People in Oxford and Banbury turned up in grand style to help towards making these unfortunate childrens' Christmas a much happier one. We understand 2,600 people paid for admission – that was grand! Headington can be congratulated on doing a fine job, everything was organised very well indeed. What a pity the weather had to be so unkind – snow lying thick on the ground made things very difficult for the players. Yet the game itself was very entertaining, players thoroughly enjoyed themselves and proved what fine fellows they are by providing first class entertainment. Risks did not mean a thing, their idea was to entertain all the good folks who kindly came along and supported the cause. A most enjoyable evening. Is there a future for football under flood-lighting? We feel there is, but time will tell."

The issue of floodlighting for the Spencer Stadium was raised at the club's AGM in 1953. Secretary/Manager Jimmy Cringan in reply to a question stated that the club were in negotiation with the Midlands Electricity Board and as soon as they could afford it they would have floodlighting installed. He said that the estimated cost was between £1,500 and £2,000.

Financial pressures though prevented flood-lighting ever happening in the lifetime of Banbury Spencer Football Club and it was not until 1966 that the Spencer Stadium got floodlighting when Spencer's successor club Banbury United installed them for their first season of Southern League football. Spencer did play some competitive games away under floodlights though, their first on Saturday 22nd December 1956 when they won 1-0 at Brierley Hill Alliance in a Birmingham Combination game.

Programme Cover Season 1950/51.

The floodlit friendly game against Headington United had been a welcome break from the routine of league fixtures but a third consecutive season of mid-table mediocrity in the Combination had taken its toll on attendances. The Club's AGM in the summer of 1951 reported that attendances had fallen from an average of 1,950 the previous season to 1,300 during the season just gone, consequently gate income was down by around £700. The club would have lost a sum of £1,269 on the year if it had not been for a donation of £900 from the Supporters Club which reduced the loss down to £369.

Chairman of the club, J.A. Deacon, commented "It would break my heart to see us lose Birmingham Combination football in Banbury. We must realise this has been brought about by Mr and Mrs Allen, No one knows how much money they had put up to get this club in Banbury going." Of the joint presidents, Jimmy Cringan added "Banbury cannot support a professional football club without Mr and Mrs Robert Allen. They have given a colossal sum."

Gil (Gilbert) Williams, Spencer's centre half, was appointed captain of the side in November 1950, taking over from Doug Woodward who retired through health problems. Gill played for Harvills Hawthorn before joining West Bromwich Albion in February 1944. He played 6 games for the Albion in War Time competition in season 1943/44, 21 in season 1944/45 and made one appearance for them in the post-War regionalised competition of season 1945/46. Though the Football League competition proper started up again in season 1946/47, Gil had to wait until season 1947/48 to make his Football League debut, making a total of seven league appearances that season for the then Second Division side, though those were to be the last league games that he played for Albion. He joined Banbury Spencer for the start of season 1949/50 and stayed with the club for two seasons, leaving in the summer of 1951 to join Darlaston after making a total of 78 first team appearances.

Season 1951/52 was one of mediocrity for Spencer. League form was indifferent from the start with the club in mid-table for the first half of the campaign. The FA Cup brought no joy either as though Spencer had a relatively easy first qualifying round FA Cup 2-1 home win over Spartan League side Huntley & Palmers, the next round was an embarrassment as Delphian League amateur side Aylesbury United left the Spencer Stadium with a convincing 4-0 win.

However, the second half of the season got worse for Spencer as after beating Dudley Town 3-2 at home on Saturday 15th December 1951, the club then only won one game from then through until losing 2-0 away to Hednesford on Saturday 22nd March 1952. At this point Spencer were down in 18th place out of 20 clubs.

Gil Williams

Birmingham Combination Table 1951/52 As at Saturday 22nd March 1952 Bottom 7				
	P	W	D	L	PTS
Bilston	31	9	8	14	26
Rugby Town	31	9	6	16	24
Moor Green	29	9	6	14	24
Bedworth Town	29	9	4	16	22
Banbury Spencer	31	8	6	17	22
Atherstone Town	30	9	2	19	20
Sutton Town	33	3	3	27	9

Banbury Spencer V Aylesbury United

"We got the bird

We had looked forward to a savoury meal of Aylesbury Duck last Saturday, but the duck proved a tough bird, and the only duck we got was in the cricket sense (and we lost by a "cricket score" at that!) Aylesbury played a fine game and surprised us intensely. We have no alibis to offer, the better team won, and that was that! We wish Aylesbury the best of luck and progress with both cups in which they are interested - the F.A. Cup and the F.A.Amateur Cup.

FOOTNOTE: We spent the following Monday engaged in the legendary Banbury pursuit of hanging cats. Our somewhat wry thought was that we were the mice!

- but finished up in the soup"

From the Spencer v Redditch programme, Saturday 20th October 1951, the week after Spencer had lost 4-0 at home to Aylesbury United in the FA Cup.

Aylesbury went on to beat Wycombe Wanderers and Hendon in the remaining qualifying rounds to reach the First Round, losing 5-0 at home to Watford.

Results did improve after this as the club picked up 11 points out of their last 14 and climbed up to finish in 15th place, though this was still Spencer's lowest finish in the Birmingham Combination since becoming members back in season 1935/36.

Goalkeeper Frank McCormack, right back Jesse Quinney and forward Joey Wilson were all ever present in Spencer's first team games during season 1951/52.

Spencer's improvement in form at the end of the season had coincided with the arrival of Les Latham as player/coach. He made his Spencer debut in a 2-2 draw at Bromsgrove Rovers at the beginning of April 1952 and after this the club picked up another 8 points out of a possible 10 in their remaining league games. Les was a central defender who had been a professional with Aston Villa, without making a first team appearance, before joining Coventry City in October 1946 as a part-time professional making one Football League appearance for them in season 1946/47. After spending three seasons at Highfield Road he took up his first coaching appointment at Lockheed Leamington. Les played for Spencer until October 1955 but

Birmingham Combination Final Table 1951/52							
	P	W	D	L	F	A	PTS
Stourbridge	38	28	6	4	99	49	62
Redditch	38	24	8	6	112	58	56
Hednesford	38	23	5	10	92	48	51
Nuneaton Borough	38	22	7	9	109	75	51
Bromsgrove Rovers	38	19	4	15	73	62	42
Tamworth	38	18	6	14	92	91	42
Stafford Rangers	38	16	9	13	83	72	41
Walsall Reserves	38	18	4	16	100	89	40
Lockheed Leamington	38	16	7	15	80	71	39
Dudley Town	38	15	7	16	67	74	37
Moor Green	38	14	7	17	71	80	35
Hinckley Athletic	38	16	3	19	60	84	35
Darlaston	38	15	4	19	77	84	34
Rugby Town	38	13	7	18	69	73	33
Banbury Spencer	38	13	7	18	76	87	33
WBA "A"	38	12	7	19	64	74	31
Bilston	38	11	9	18	74	111	31
Bedworth Town	38	12	6	20	89	88	30
Atherstone Town	38	11	3	24	64	103	25
Sutton Town	38	4	4	30	40	118	12

then continued with the club in a coaching capacity until quitting three weeks before the end of the 1955/56 season to move back to Lockheed Leamington as their manager.

At the club's AGM in July 1952 the Chairman, J.A. Deacon, reported that without the aid of £1,400 received from the Supporters Club and a £500 donation from the President, Robert Allen, it would have been impossible for the club to continue. A deficit on the season of £1,006 would have occurred without those donations. The Treasurer Eric Lowe stated that crowds averaging 2,000 were needed to keep the club in the clear but during the past season there had only been eight games where that was achieved. The average for the season was a little under 1,500 and at times the gate had fallen to 700. The Chairman of the Supporters Club, Mr W.R. Stroud, blamed a "get our money's worth" spirit in Banburians as part of the reason for the club's financial misfortunes.

Season 1952/3 did not begin well. An exit from the FA Cup to Maidenhead United in the Preliminary Round was a disappointment, a 1-1 draw at the Spencer Stadium being followed by a 3-0 defeat in Berkshire. A run of five consecutive league defeats from Saturday 27th September 1952 to Saturday 1st November 1952 left the club one from bottom of the table with just four points from nine games. Results continued to be poor from this point through to Saturday 24th January 1953 when

Spencer lost 2-1 away to West Bromwich Albion "A", the club gaining just three wins in this period. After the West Bromwich Albion game Spencer were bottom of the table, with 10 points from 18 games.

Birmingham Combination Table 1952/53 As at Saturday 24th January 1953 – Bottom 4	P	W	D	L	F	A	PTS
Tamworth	17	4	5	8	22	34	13
Lockheed Leamington	20	5	3	12	25	43	13
Sutton Town	22	3	5	14	28	64	11
Banbury Spencer	18	4	2	12	30	40	10

The poor form in the first half of the season had resulted in a large fall in attendances and consequently the club was experiencing financial problems. Just before Christmas, with recent gates of 881, 638 and 853, well under half of the support necessary to keep the club going, the players agreed unanimously to accept a £1 per match reduction in pay. The player/coach Les Latham volunteered to accept a £2 a week reduction in his salary. Secretary/ Manager Jimmy Cringan commented "This is a direct contradiction of the charge often brought against the professional footballer that he is in the game only for the money."

There was a further development concerning the poor form and financial issues at the beginning of January 1953 when at a joint meeting of the Football Club and Supporters Club committees, the Football Club offered the Supporters Club the chance to take over Banbury Spencer Football Club as a town club. A subsequent meeting of the committee of the Supporters Club on Tuesday January 13th 1953 declined the offer and they issued a statement to say that after a long discussion it was agreed that to run it as a town team would be even more expensive than it is now and that their view was that both committees should continue to work together for the same objective of a good class of football in Banbury. The Supporters Club announced that they would hand over immediately the sum of £400 to the football club.

Results for the season did improve significantly from the end of January 1953 onwards. The club's final 16 league games saw 20 points gained and this was enough for Spencer to climb up the table and finish in 13th place out of the 18 teams with 30 points from 34 games.

Leading league goalscorer for Spencer in season 1952/53, with 17 goals, was centre-forward Ted Roberts who was one of the most experienced former Football League players to have played for the Spencer Club in their history. Ted joined Derby County from Glapwell Colliery in April 1934 and made his Football League debut on March 7th 1936 playing at inside left in a Division One game at West Bromwich Albion, retaining his place in the side for the next three games. However, these were to be his last appearances for the Rams before moving to Coventry City in March 1937. His best footballing days were probably lost due to the War but nevertheless he made 211 Football League appearances

Ted Roberts

for Coventry between seasons 1936/37 and 1951/52 scoring 85 goals. He moved to King's Lynn in the summer of 1952 but in September of that year he joined Banbury Spencer, scoring a hat-trick on his debut in a 5-2 win over West Bromwich Albion "A". Ted topped the Spencer league goalscorers list in both seasons 1952/53 and 1953/54. In the case of the latter season despite his moving to Bedworth Town in early February of 1954 in an exchange deal for Jack Evans. His Spencer career saw him make a total of 60 first team appearances for the club, scoring 41 goals.

Birmingham Combination Final Table 1952/53							
	P	W	D	L	F	A	PTS
Redditch	34	21	7	6	84	60	49
Hednesford	34	20	6	8	81	46	46
Stourbridge	34	19	3	12	71	57	41
Rugby Town	34	16	8	10	64	38	40
Bilston	34	16	6	12	75	61	38
Atherstone Town	34	14	9	11	85	75	37
Dudley Town	34	17	2	15	67	71	36
Moor Green	34	16	4	14	64	70	36
Bromsgrove Rovers	34	12	11	11	65	79	35
Hinckley Athletic	34	14	6	14	67	69	34
Walsall Reserves	34	11	11	12	56	57	33
Darlaston	34	14	3	17	53	59	31
Banbury Spencer	34	12	6	16	73	65	30
Tamworth	34	11	8	15	55	64	30
Lockheed Leamington	34	10	6	18	56	68	26
Sutton Town	34	9	6	19	44	84	24
WBA "A"	34	10	3	21	54	73	23
Bedworth Town	34	9	5	20	49	67	23

Though crowds had been very low in the couple of months prior to Christmas 1952, the club's improved form from the start of the year plus the better weather had from this point a beneficial effect on the numbers entering through the Spencer turnstiles. The club's AGM in the summer of 1953 reported an average attendance for the season of 1,502, marginally up on the previous year. This did not though mean that it had been a good year financially. Expenditure had been £3,279 against income of £2,205 (£1,073 of the income coming from gate receipts) giving a basic loss of £1,074. The loss was though reduced to £374 by donations from the Supporters Club and the newly formed Britannia Club.

December 1952 had seen the "Britannia Club" set up, a Supporters weekly competition to raise money for the benefit of the Football Club. Agents were paid a commission based on the amount of cash collected on a weekly basis. The club made the following statement in the programme for the game against Dudley Town on Saturday 22nd November 1952, under the heading "Britannia Club": "The above club has been formed to raise money for the benefit of professional football in Banbury. It could not have been formed under the name of Banbury Spencer Football Club or Banbury Spencer Supporters Club – hence the reason for the name "Britannia Club". The article added that the promoters would be former players Dick Pike and Arthur Blencowe, as well as current Secretary/Manager Jimmy Cringan and appealed for agents, emphasising that agents would find the scheme a source of income due to the weekly commission paid to them. "Floodlighting is the aim – Join up and ensure floodlighting at the Stadium", the statement added.

Though floodlighting was never achieved in the lifetime of Banbury Spencer, it is fair to say that the amount of money raised by supporters and the local public through the "Britannia Club" played a huge part in the continuation of professional football in Banbury for many years. As an example season 1954/55 saw the sum of £4,250 donated by the "Britannia Club" to the Football Club, equal today in 2013 to approximately £90,000.

CHAPTER 14

FA Intermediate Cup

In the club's programme for the Birmingham Combination game against Bedworth Town on Saturday 11th March 1950, Spencer stated their intention to make a case for the introduction of an FA Cup for "non-league" professional clubs with a final at Wembley.

Part of Spencer's concerns were as a result of their being drawn away in the past to small amateur clubs with low crowds in the early rounds of the FA Cup which led to heavy financial losses. One of Spencer's key arguments was that a competition for just the professional non-League clubs would attract much larger crowds thus avoiding these losses, as well as giving supporters of such clubs a much more realistic chance of seeing their team at Wembley.

Spencer summarised their argument as follows "League clubs and amateur clubs have the chance to take their followers to Wembley. Why shouldn't clubs in our class of football have the same chance?"

Recognising that clubs at this time competed in the FA Cup and County Cups as well as league programmes, thus having a very full schedule, and that it might therefore be difficult for them to compete in another competition, Spencer put forward for consideration the following:

1. FA Cup – to be competed for by Football League clubs only and the eight quarter finalists from the previous season's FA Intermediate Cup

2. FA Intermediate Cup – to be competed for by non-league semi-professional clubs and the eight quarter finalists from the previous season's FA Amateur Cup

3. FA Amateur Cup – to be competed for by amateur clubs

   All three competitions were to have finals at Wembley.

A further statement on the issue appeared in the club's programme two weeks later which read "We, Banbury Spencer FC, fully realise this suggestion has been discussed at one time or another by almost every professional club outside League football. We do not claim to have originated the idea, but it required a club to start the ball rolling. Actually, in publicly drawing attention to it, our club was offering itself as a "sounding board", and took the responsibility to circulate clubs and organise a meeting. The chance is now within sight to make the dream of having a National Trophy which one of the minor professional clubs can actually win, a reality."

Secretary/Manager Jimmy Cringan had a meeting at Lancaster Gate with Sir Stanley Rous, Secretary of the English FA. As a result of this meeting a memorandum was sent out by the FA to all relevant clubs for their views.

A useful summary of the issues can be seen from the following article which appeared under the heading "Varying Views on Special Cup for Non-League Clubs Idea" in the Hull Daily Mail on 27th April 1950:

"Last word has not yet been said about the proposal to form an FA Intermediate Cup competition for non-League clubs. Although repre-sentatives from 13 minor professional leagues supported the scheme outlined by Banbury Spencer at the recent meeting in Birmingham, a number of clubs are known to oppose the idea. Mr Arthur Mortimer, chairman of the progressive Southern League, says "We want the time and the opportunity to discuss this proposed competition before we advise our members what course they should adopt." One leading Southern League club official expresses the view that teams outside the Football League rely on two main sources of income, other than their own gate receipts. They are transfer fees and a successful run in the FA Cup. To exclude all but a few non-League sides from the senior tournament might seriously affect the financial status of smaller clubs. Such clubs as Yeovil, Gillingham and Colchester United, who have done so well in the FA Cup competition since the war, may feel that the disadvantages of the new plan outweigh its advantages."

Whilst most of the minor professional leagues had been in favour, the Southern League duly came out against the idea. It is understandable that some of their clubs were concerned at missing out on money spinning FA Cup games against Football League clubs – as the top league in semi-professional football their teams were at this time most likely to make it through to the Competition Proper and therefore to not be able to enter the FA Cup but instead have to compete in the FA Intermediate Cup was a financial concern to such clubs.

After receiving feedback to the suggestion, Sir Stanley Rous wrote to the Banbury Spencer club in December 1950 as follows: "Whilst the views of the professional clubs outside the Football League are appreciated, particularly the frequency with which clubs lose financially as a result of being drawn against small amateur clubs in the early rounds of the FA Challenge Competition, it was agreed that the time has not yet come to introduce the sweeping changes outlined in the Memorandum. I would assure you, however, that the idea of introducing a new Intermediate Cup Competition has not been dismissed, and that future meetings will be held to give further consideration to the proposal."

Spencer's comment on the FA's letter was as follows: "FA Intermediate Cup, which would have created new interest in our class of football, would have been a great build up from a financial angle and most professional clubs outside the football league are beginning to realise something is required. It is essential we have our own cup with a final at Wembley. Let us stick together and make the suggestion a reality. The FA are sympathetic towards our suggestion – let us prove to them we are wholehearted for a FA Intermediate Cup."

Spencer did not let the matter rest at this point. Season 1951/52 saw them carry out their own survey of non League professional clubs to ascertain the support for such a competition with the results forwarded to the FA. At the end of December 1951 the club reported that results of the survey showed 102 clubs in favour with 29 against, though those against one would have expected to have included the bigger and most influential non League clubs.

Nearly three years later in the club's programme for the game against Boldmere St Michaels on Tuesday 14th September 1954, Spencer made further comment on the possible introduction of such a competition, when discussing a 3-0 away win at Huntley & Palmers of Reading in the FA Cup Preliminary Round on the previous Saturday. It was firstly pointed out that the attendance of 162 was the lowest at any ground that Spencer had visited since becoming a senior club, including their Oxfordshire Senior League days, demonstrating how costly it could be, with wages to pay, to compete in the early rounds of the FA Cup. The club finished with the following statement "What a difference it would make to gate receipts should professional clubs outside League football have their own National Trophy put up by the Football Association?" adding, presumably sarcastically, "Our guess is that this Trophy will be put up for competition in about 1960."

In fact it turned out that Spencer were being rather optimistic in forecasting the start date. Nearly 20 years elapsed before it took effect when the FA Trophy was introduced from season 1969/70. Of course, by this time most semi-professional clubs of a decent standard had floodlights, so it was much easier to fit extra games into the schedules and there was now no question of clubs entering the Trophy being unable to enter the FA Cup, the stumbling block to the proposal back in 1950. Sadly, by the time the FA Trophy came into being, Banbury Spencer Football Club were no more. However, successor club Banbury United, due to Spencer's original proposals back in the early 1950s, always claimed a special affinity with the competition in its early days and had some minor success in the 1970s, reaching the last 16 in season 1970/71 and also in 1973/74.

CHAPTER 15

Oxfordshire Professional Cup

With Headington United having turned professional when joining the Southern League in the summer of 1949, the Oxfordshire FA made the decision a couple of years later to put up a trophy which could be competed for by the County's now two professional clubs. Thus the Oxfordshire Professional Cup was introduced for season 1951/52 and so Headington United and Banbury Spencer met on an annual basis right through until Spencer's final season of football in 1964/65.

The first season saw the clubs toss for the right to host the game and this was won by Headington. The inaugural game took place at the Manor Ground on Saturday May 10th 1952 witnessed by a crowd estimated at between 5,000 and 6,000.

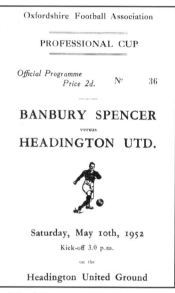

The game was packed with goals. Headington scored in the first minute but within ten minutes Spencer were 2-1 in front through goals from Joey Wilson and Archie Crilly. However, just two minutes after going behind Headington were level once more and soon scored again to take a 3-2 lead before Dicky Howe netted for Spencer to tie the game up 3-3, all six goals thus far having come in the first 21 minutes of the game. There were no more goals in the remainder of the half. Headington had much the better of the opening stages of the second half and had added two more goals before half of the period had gone to give them a 5-3 lead. However, in the 80th minute Spencer reduced the deficit to one goal when Johnny North scored but, though Spencer were now right back in the game, they were unable to find an equaliser in the last ten minutes so it was Headington United who became the first winners of the Oxfordshire Professional Cup.

The Spencer line up was, Frank McCormack, Jesse Quinney, Joe Greszik, Ernest Ryman, Les Latham, Phil Zambra, Joey Wilson, Dick Howe, John North, Norman Brison, and Archie Crilly.

Seasons 1952/53 to 1956/57 saw the cup decided on a home and away basis before it reverted to a one game format from season 1957/58.

Season 1952/53 thus saw the first game between the sides in this competition at the Spencer Stadium. Headington arrived for the first leg on Tuesday 5th May 1953 as Southern League Champions and had clearly, in just a few years, overtaken Spencer to become the premier professional football club in Oxfordshire. The local football public of Banbury were certainly, at least in its early days, attracted to this new competition with 3,169 in attendance for the game, the biggest crowd of the season at the Spencer Stadium. Headington led 1-0 at the interval and should have made it 2-0 early in the second half but Spencer goalkeeper Frank McCormack pulled off an excellent save from a Johnny Crichton penalty kick. Spencer equalised when a bout of inter-passing between Dicky Meadows, Ray Hagar and Ted Roberts ended with Roberts shooting past the Headington goalkeeper. Spencer went near to clinching the game in the closing stages when first Joey Wilson had a shot headed off the line and then Colin Whetton went close when he had only the goalkeeper to beat but with neither side scoring further goals the game finished 1-1.

The Spencer line up was, Frank McCormack, Jesse Quinney, Archie Crilly, Dick Howe, Les Latham, Ernest Ryman, Joey Wilson, Ted Roberts, Ray Hagar, Colin Whetton and Dicky Meadows.

Spencer put up an even better performance in the away leg four days later. There was a crowd of between 5,000 and 6,000 at the Manor Ground which included a fair sprinkling of Spencer supporters. Headington fielded their full Southern League side.

The Spencer line up for the second leg showed two changes in personnel from the first leg with Phil Zambra coming in for Les Latham and Doug McPhee for Dicky Meadows.

NOTES

Oxfordshire's two professional football clubs, Banbury Spencer and Headington United, meet this afternoon to decide the destiny of the Oxfordshire Professional Cup for the next twelve months. This is only the second year this trophy has been offered, and Headington are the holders. In the first leg on Tuesday, following a very enjoyable game, the match was drawn 1—1, so both teams take the field this afternoon all square.

As Banbury Spencer showed quite clearly on Tuesday, they have not felt any inferiority complex when faced with the Southern League Champions and Southern League Cup-winners, another good game can be anticipated, which says much for the spirit of the Banbury club, who have always been admired when visiting Manor Road. It was pleasing to note that a 3,000 crowd watched Tuesday evening's game, and should a similar 5,000 crowd be here this afternoon, as attended last year, then a considerable 'gate' will have been brought about by the introduction of this trophy game. The proceeds are shared three ways, with the O.F.A. and the two clubs. The Oxfordshire F.A. will therefore benefit by a good sum from professional football for the continued operation of Association football in Oxfordshire.

Extract from Headington United v Banbury Spencer programme Saturday 9th May 1953.

The game was goalless at half time but Spencer went ahead early in the second half when a corner taken by Ray Hagar saw the ball drop into the goalmouth and then get pushed back to Ted Roberts who fired in a terrific shot which gave the Headington goalkeeper no chance. It didn't take long for Headington to equalise but with no further goals in the second half and with the scores 2-2 on aggregate, the game went into extra time. The additional 30 minutes saw both Colin Whetton and Ted Roberts have good shots saved by the Headington goalkeeper and Ray Hagar missed what looked to be a certain winner for Spencer when, with just the goalkeeper to beat, he shot tamely into the custodian's hands.

However, with no goals in extra time, the cup was therefore to be shared for a year with Spencer having the honour of bringing the cup back to Banbury on the

Saturday night after winning the toss for who should have it for the first six months.

Season 1952/53 though proved to be the nearest that Spencer came to winning this cup outright in their history. Headington, or later Oxford United as they became known from season 1960/61, confirmed their status as the county's top professional club by winning it every season from this point on through until, and including, Spencer's final season of football in 1964/65.

Oxford United's success was noted in their programme for the final of the 1961 competition when they wrote "With the exception of one season, when honours were shared, we have had the good fortune to keep the trophy at the Manor since its inception, and it has become virtually part of the "furniture" in the Boardroom, but we do think the time is fast approaching when Jimmy will have to do something about getting it to Banbury for twelve months, if only to give us a "break" from keeping it clean."

Oxfordshire Professional Cup
Banbury Spencer v Headington United/Oxford United

	Home	Away		Home	Away
1951/52		L 4-5	1958/59	L 0-2	
1952/53	D 1-1	D 1-1	1959/60		L 0-3
1953/54	L 1-2	L 1-3	1960/61		L 0-2
1954/55	D 2-2	L 2-3	1961/62		L 2-4
1955/56	D 1-1	L 1-4	1962/63	L 2-3	
1956/57	L 1-2	L 2-6	1963/64		L 2-8
1957/58		L 1-2	1964/65	L 0-5	

CHAPTER 16

From the Birmingham Combination to the Birmingham League

By the early 1950s the Birmingham Combination, of which Banbury Spencer were members, and the rival Birmingham League were considered to be of roughly equal strength. The first signs of a possible change in this status occurred in the summer of 1952 when Nuneaton Borough, who had finished fourth in the Combination table in 1951/52, and Stafford Rangers who had finished seventh, opted to leave to join the Birmingham League and Cheshire County League respectively.

Nuneaton's defection was influenced by the Combination's decision not to rescind the rule of a maximum player wage of £3 per match. This limit was intended to allow clubs with smaller resources to compete on a more equal footing with those with much larger resources. Nuneaton felt this was a restriction which prevented them from providing their supporters with the best possible football. There was no such wage limit in either the Birmingham League or Cheshire County League and, though Stafford Rangers stated their move was influenced by a desire to enable their supporters to see some new teams, both clubs probably felt that their new leagues offered more scope without the limit.

With no replacements, the Combination was reduced to 18 clubs for season 1952/53.

February 1953 saw the Birmingham League propose a merger with the Combination. This was considered by the Combination clubs at a meeting on Thursday 26th February but was rejected by twelve votes to six. Banbury Spencer was one of the clubs to vote against the merger. Their view, stated in club programme notes, was that if the Midlands based Southern League and Cheshire League clubs had agreed to come in to form a really strong First Division then they would have voted for the merger but without this they saw no benefit, either from a playing or financial point of view.

The "fall out" of the decision to reject the merger was almost immediate with Stourbridge, Redditch and Hednesford who had finished first, second and third in the Combination in season 1951/52, being joined by Dudley Town, Bromsgrove Rovers and Walsall Reserves in giving notice that they would be resigning from the Combination to join the Birmingham League for the start of season 1953/54. The loss of these six clubs was a serious set-back to the Combination for though Gresley Rovers and Birch Coppice were new teams added; these were some way short of the quality and spectator drawing power of the clubs that they had lost. The Birmingham League was clearly now the stronger of the two competitions.

With six clubs leaving and only two joining, this reduced the Combination down to 14 clubs for season 1953/54 which was far from satisfactory and only gave clubs 26 league games, not enough for a full season of fixtures. The Combination therefore decided to introduce an additional competition for the end of the season and put up the "Tillotson Cup" for the winners. The competition was in effect a re-run of the league season but with clubs playing one another just the once.

Spencer made a good start to season 1953/54. A home game in the Preliminary Round of the FA Cup to top amateur side Wycombe Wanderers attracted 3,150 spectators and most were not to be disappointed with Spencer's display as goals from Ken Clark and Colin Whetton gave them a 2-1 win. Spencer's reward was a First Qualifying Round home derby game against Oxford City, another Isthmian League side. An even larger crowd than for the previous round, 4,327, turned out to see Spencer win 2-0, the goals coming from a Bernard Brock penalty and Colin Whetton. After those two performances a 1-0 defeat away to Corinthian League Chesham United in the next round was a disappointment but at least the season's competition had created local interest and benefited the club financially.

Spencer's league campaign also began with a lot of promise, winning four of their first five games. Results continued to be good and after a 2-1 away win to Sutton Town on Saturday 21st November 1953, the club had lost just two Combination games and, having gained 19 points from 13 games, were in third place in the table.

Meanwhile, a meeting of Combination clubs on Thursday 19th November 1953 had voted to bring themselves into line with the Birmingham League by abolishing, from the start of the following season, the £3 a match wage limit. Spencer secretary/manager Jimmy Cringan, who proposed the abolition, which was seconded by Atherstone Town, speaking in favour of the motion said he thought it would encourage more clubs to join the league. Three clubs voted against but ironically that was because they wanted it abolished immediately. All clubs agreed that the Combination needed to be strengthened in numbers. At this time there were strong rumours that several Combination clubs intended to apply for membership of the Birmingham League for the following season. When questioned on this issue Jimmy Cringan told the Banbury Guardian that he had heard nothing of it and did not believe there was any truth in the rumour. He said Banbury Spencer were definitely not considering leaving for the Birmingham League.

Despite losing at home to Darlaston at the end of November and away to Atherstone at the beginning of December, Spencer responded positively to these set-backs to pick up five

Birmingham Combination Table 1953/54 As at Saturday 21st November 1953 - Top 4							
	P	W	D	L	F	A	PTS
Bilston	13	10	2	1	33	15	22
Atherstone Town	16	8	5	3	42	26	21
Banbury Spencer	13	8	3	2	27	16	19
Rugby Town	12	9	0	3	31	17	18

Birmingham Combination Table 1953/54 As at Saturday 2nd January 1954 - Top 6							
	P	W	D	L	F	A	PTS
Bilston	19	12	5	2	54	25	29
Atherstone Town	21	11	7	3	53	34	29
Rugby Town	18	11	2	5	41	25	24
Banbury Spencer	18	10	4	4	37	24	24
Hinckley Athletic	19	6	9	4	32	24	21
Tamworth	22	8	5	9	45	42	21

points from their remaining three games in December and were still in touch with the league leaders after games played on Saturday 2nd January 1954, being in fourth place with 24 points from 18 games, five points behind leaders Bilston but with a game in hand on them.

Programme Cover Season 1953/54.

Major developments occurred in terms of the Birmingham Combination and Birmingham League in February 1954. The low number of teams in the Combination was now of increasing concern to all its members and at a league meeting, Spencer secretary/manager Jimmy Cringan stated "If any more clubs go out of the Combination we shall have to make application for the Birmingham League. It is our duty to provide the best possible football for Banbury supporters." Clubs did indeed decide after that meeting to leave and Jimmy Cringan confirmed Spencer's resignation from the Combination to the Banbury Advertiser on Wednesday 17th February 1954. 13 of the 14 clubs in the Combination for season 1953/54 duly applied to join the Birmingham League for the start of the following season and were accepted at a February Birmingham League meeting, the only non applicants were West Bromwich Albion "A". The Combination secretary now suggested that the leagues amalgamate but as 13 of the 14 Combination clubs had applied to join the Birmingham League directly this was rejected, though of course in practical terms this is what happened, albeit not in name.

Meanwhile clubs were completing their Combination fixtures for season 1953/54. Though Spencer had been "in touch" with the leaders at the turn of the year, the eight points that Spencer got from their final eight league games were not enough to see the club mount a late challenge for the Championship. Their final total of 32 points from 26 games earned them 4th place out of the 14 clubs.

The Tillotson Cup at the end of the season began well for Spencer as they picked up 8 points from their first 5 games. However, with only one win in their remaining 8 games the club slipped right down the table to finish in 11th place out of the 14 clubs with just 11 points from 13 games.

A notable debutant for Spencer in season 1953/54 was forward Jack Evans who joined the club in early February of 1954 from

Birmingham Combination Final Table 1953/54							
	P	W	D	L	F	A	PTS
Rugby Town	26	17	3	6	64	35	37
Bilston	26	14	6	6	67	37	34
Atherstone Town	26	13	7	6	60	42	33
Banbury Spencer	26	14	4	8	50	36	32
Lockheed Leamington	26	13	5	8	50	27	31
Hinckley Athletic	26	9	10	7	41	39	28
Tamworth	26	11	5	10	53	49	27
Bedworth Town	26	10	6	10	45	54	26
Gresley Rovers	26	10	4	12	65	58	24
WBA "A"	26	10	4	12	46	50	24
Darlaston	26	9	5	12	42	47	23
Birch Coppice Colliery	26	6	9	11	37	57	21
Moor Green	26	5	5	16	32	61	15
Sutton Town	26	3	3	20	32	92	9

Bedworth Town with Ted Roberts going the other way in an exchange deal. Co-incidentally Jack had been the understudy for a number of years to Roberts at Coventry City after joining them as a professional in May 1947. Jack progressed to make eight Football League appearances for Coventry between seasons 1948/49 and 1950/51 inclusive and scored one goal for them, that goal coming on his debut for the club in a 1-0 win at Highfield Road over Fulham in a Division 2 game in early April 1949. After leaving Coventry City in 1952, Jack had played for Nuneaton Borough and Rugby Town as well as Bedworth Town prior to joining Spencer. From joining Spencer in

Jack Evans

February 1954 to the end of that season, Jack played at centre forward making 18 appearances and scoring 9 goals. The following three seasons saw Jack show his versatility by playing in all the forward positions, including on the two wings, except inside right. He was Spencer's leading league goalscorer in both seasons 1955/56 and 1956/57. After making a total of 134 appearances for Banbury Spencer between February 1954 and November 1957, scoring 65 goals, he left the club, playing for Lockheed Leamington for a number of seasons.

With such an influx of teams from the Birmingham Combination, the Birmingham League now had a total of 40 clubs for season 1954/55. The League made the decision to split the teams into two divisions of 20 clubs, a Southern Division and a Northern Division. The top ten clubs from each division at the end of the season would then form a First Division for season 1955/56 with the bottom ten forming a Second Division. Promotion and relegation would subsequently operate between the divisions.

The 20 teams in the Southern Division for season 1954/55 were as follows:

Aston Villa "A"	Dudley Town	Redditch
Banbury Spencer	Halesowen Town	Rugby Town
Boldmere St Michaels	Hereford United Res	Stourbridge
Brierley Hill Alliance	Kidderminster Harriers Res	Sutton Town
Bromsgrove Rovers	Lockheed Leamington	Symingtons (M. Harborough)
Cheltenham Town Res	Lye Town	Worcester City Res
Cradley Heath	Moor Green	

At Banbury Spencer's AGM held in August 1954, the hope was expressed that the club's new adventure into the Birmingham League would be a success. Secretary/Manager Jimmy Cringan stated "We shall do everything to achieve our aim of finishing in the top half of the League". He added that players would in future be paid a £1 bonus for a win and 10 shillings bonus for a drawn match "We feel players should be given some incentive to go all out to win. That is why we are endeavouring to pay a bonus."

Treasurer Eric Lowe, at the AGM, stated that the average gate of 1,450 for the season had been 50 less than the season before. The figure of 1,450 had though been favourably enhanced by the large attendances for the two home FA Cup games against Wycombe Wanderers and Oxford City. Crowds towards the end of the season were poor with the Tillotson Cup in particular not being greeted by Spencer supporters with much enthusiasm.

Consistent with Jimmy Cringan's statement at the AGM that the club was doing everything possible to ensure a good first season in the Birmingham League, three players with Football League experience were signed prior to the start of the season. These were centre-forward Barry (real name Brinley) Thomas who was signed from Coventry City after making 12 Football League appearances for the Sky Blues over the previous two seasons, inside right Tommy McGarrity who had made 5 Football League appearances for Southampton before spending the previous season playing for Southern League Headington United and left winger Jimmy Bradley who had appeared in the Football League for Shrewsbury Town as well as having a Scottish League Cup final appearance to his name for Hibernian against Motherwell at Hampden Park in front of a crowd of 64,074, oddly his only first team appearance for the Scottish club.

Spencer's new adventure into Birming-ham League football began with a trip to Bromsgrove Rovers on Saturday 21st August 1954 and it was an excellent start with goals from Tommy McGarrity, Colin Whetton, Barry Thomas and Ralph Tallis giving the Gay Puritans a 4-0 win. Though Spencer lost on the following Tuesday 2-1 at home to

Birmingham League Southern Division Table 1954/55 As at Saturday 16th October 1954 - Top 6							
	P	W	D	L	F	A	PTS
Redditch	8	6	2	0	20	4	14
Brierley Hill Alliance	10	6	2	2	29	16	14
Banbury Spencer	8	6	1	1	19	5	13
Bromsgrove Rovers	10	6	1	3	32	15	13
Worcester City Res	9	5	2	2	22	10	12
Lockheed Leamington	9	5	2	2	22	10	12

Leamington, they responded to that defeat by going on an unbeaten league run of 6 games, including five wins, culminating in a 2-1 win at Moor Green on Saturday 16th October. After the Moor Green game, Spencer were in third place in the Birmingham League Southern Division with 13 points from 8 games.

Whilst the start to the Birmingham League campaign had been promising, there was disappointment in the FA Cup. Although Huntley & Palmers of Reading were comfortably beaten 3-0 away in the Preliminary Round, a 1-0 defeat at Corinthian League side Chesham United in the First Qualifying Round was to follow.

Considering Spencer's start, league form from Saturday 23rd October 1954 through to Christmas was disappointing with the club picking up just six points from the eight games that they played. After a 0-0 draw away to Stourbridge on Saturday 1st January 1955, Spencer had dropped down to 10th place with 20 points from 17 games played.

However, Spencer then went on a record breaking winning run for their days in senior football. From Saturday 22nd January 1955 through to Saturday 26th March

1955 (inclusive), Spencer won 10 consecutive Birmingham League games. After their 5-1 win at home to Symington's of Market Harborough on 26th March, Spencer's winning run had seen them climb back up to fourth place with a total of 40 points from 28 games. Redditch, the league leaders and eight points ahead of Spencer, were looking unlikely to be caught but with games in hand on the second and third placed clubs, a runners-up spot was very much in Spencer's own hands.

Despite Spencer being undefeated in their eight league games throughout the month of April, they had by the beginning of May, with just two games to go, slipped out of contention for the Southern Division Championship and for the runners-up spot as they could only win two of those games. After failing to win either of their league games in May, Spencer, in the end, had to settle for fourth place with 51 points from 38 games.

Nevertheless, though Spencer's Championship challenge had not been maintained during the closing weeks of the season, the club's priority of finishing in the top ten of the Southern Division, to ensure First Division Birmingham League football at the Spencer Stadium for season 1955/56, had been achieved. To recognise this achievement the club placed an advert in the Banbury Guardian on Thursday 5th May 1955 under the heading "A Public Appreciation", thanking the players, football management, club stalwarts and its Supporters Club.

Leading goalscorer for Spencer in season 1954/55 was centre-forward Barry Thomas who scored 22 Birmingham League goals in the 34 games in which he played. He had played for Longford Rovers before joining Coventry City in September 1950 progressing to make his Football League debut on April 3rd 1953 against Colchester United. He went on to make

Programme Cover Season 1954/55.

Birmingham League Southern Division Table 1954/55 As at Saturday 26th March 1955 - Top 7						
	P	W	D	L	F	A	PTS
Redditch	29	22	4	3	88	31	48
Lockheed Leamington	31	19	6	6	103	46	44
Worcester City Res	29	19	3	7	90	44	41
Banbury Spencer	28	18	4	6	67	30	40
Brierley Hill Alliance	27	18	3	6	84	44	39
Bromsgrove Rovers	26	14	4	8	63	41	32
Rugby Town	25	13	5	7	65	40	31

Birmingham League Southern Division Final Table 1954/55						
	P	W	D	L	F	A	PTS
Redditch	38	27	6	5	110	41	60
Lockheed Leamington	38	24	7	7	122	54	55
Brierley Hill Alliance	38	23	7	8	105	61	53
Banbury Spencer	38	20	11	7	84	42	51
Rugby Town	38	21	7	10	91	54	49
Worcester City Res	38	22	4	12	103	60	48
Stourbridge	38	21	6	11	86	56	48
Bromsgrove Rovers	38	18	8	12	77	56	44
Halesowen Town	38	20	4	14	100	84	44
Lye Town	38	18	4	16	76	72	40
Kidderminster H Res	38	17	5	16	79	83	39
Cheltenham Town Res	38	17	3	18	67	87	37
Moor Green	38	15	4	19	74	78	34
Cradley Heath	38	9	9	20	70	83	27
Hereford United Res	38	11	5	22	73	97	27
Symingtons	38	11	5	22	64	97	27
Aston Villa "A"	38	8	5	25	56	108	21
Sutton Town	38	7	6	25	53	117	20
Dudley Town	38	6	7	25	54	125	19
Boldmere St. Michaels	38	5	7	26	41	130	17

a total of 12 Football League appearances for Coventry over the course of seasons 1952/53 and 1953/54, scoring 1 goal before joining Banbury Spencer during the summer of 1954. He was not so prolific in his second season with Spencer but still notched 12 league goals. After two seasons at Banbury he moved to Bedworth Town for season 1956/57 but returned to the Spencer Stadium to play for the club in the two legs of the Oxfordshire Professional Cup final against Headington United in May 1957 of that season. He was obviously lined up for a return to the Spencer team for season 1957/58 and this duly was the case though his second stint at the Spencer Stadium was less successful for though he scored 7 goals in 14 Birmingham League games in this spell he was dropped after an away game at Bedworth on 11th January

A Public Appreciation

BANBURY SPENCER F.C., being now assured of a place in next season's First Division of THE BIRMINGHAM DISTRICT LEAGUE, wish publicly to express their appreciation of the services of the loyal and enthusiastic happy band of excellent "Club men", First Team Players: Frank McCormack, Ced Bennett, Archie Crilly, Harry Meadows, Les Latham, Mick Jenkins, Jack Evans, Tommy McGarrity, Barry Thomas, Colin Whetton, Jimmy Bradley, Dicky Howe, Brian Stone, Ralph Tallis, Geoff Richardson, Bernard Brock, Bryn Stephens, David Nicholls, John Hicks and Brian Wyatt, whose efforts were responsible for achieving this success.

BANBURY SPENCER F.C. also take this opportunity of paying their compliments to ex-stalwarts still in the Banbury area:-
Doug Woodward, Eric Lowe, Bob Kinder, Jesse Twynham, Harry Locke, Ralph Martin, Dick Pike, Jim McCarthy, Douglas McPhee, Reg Wallis, Norman Walls, "Cobbler" Grant, Dai Jones, Arthur Blencowe, Bertie Aston, Tommy Bott and "Alby" White; and also extend their best regards and sincere good wishes to old stalwarts they regret are seen at Banbury too seldom: Bill Saunders, Albert Shanks, Joe Hackett, Jack Screen, George Dudley, Phil Zambra, Frank Treagust, Herbert Hunt, Horace Ball, "Joey" Wilson, Alan Orr, Jesse Quinney, Tommy North, John North, Ernest Ryman, Bob Salmond, George Bate, Gil Williams, Wilf Walsh and Ronnie Westcott.

THE CLUB further takes this opportunity to pay tribute to its enterprising and loyal "second-to-none" SUPPORTERS' CLUB without whose financial aid the Club could not afford to operate in playing membership of the Birmingham League, and last but not least to "JIMMY" CRINGAN, ex Sunderland, Glasgow Celtic and Birmingham half-back, the Architect and Engineer of the Club's success.

Paid for notice placed by the Club in the Thursday 5th May 1955 edition of the Banbury Guardian

1958 and relegated to the reserves. In February he informed the club that he wished to move to Rugby Town and this request was agreed. He later played for Redditch and Tamworth.

Season 1954/55 had seen left back Archie Crilly and goalkeeper Frank McCormack make the maximum possible 47 first team appearances for Spencer. Right back Cedric Bennett and right half-back Harry Meadows both missed just the one game.

At the club's AGM in July 1955, it was announced that, thanks to donations of £4,250 from the Spencer Supporters competition the "Britannia Club", the Football Club had made a small profit of £63. Despite the successful season on the field, average gates had fallen to 1,432 a drop of 27 from the previous season, albeit this season had seen no large FA Cup attendances as there had been the season before which had then boosted up the average. The Treasurer Eric Lowe found this rather disappointing.

Secretary/manager Jimmy Cringan in his address to the meeting said "We had an exceptionally good season last year, when we achieved our major ambition of finishing in the top ten of the Birmingham League Southern Division, assuring ourselves of a place in Division 1 for next season." He then paid tribute to the success of player/coach Les Latham in building a first class side with a fine and happy team spirit.

Action from the Spencer Stadium as Barry Thomas heads the ball towards goal.

For season 1955/56, the top ten sides from the Southern and Northern Divisions formed the Birmingham League's First Division. The 20 teams were as follows:

Banbury Spencer	Halesowen Town	Shrewsbury Town Reserves
Bedworth Town	Hinckley Athletic	Stourbridge
Bilston	Lockheed Leamington	Walsall Reserves
Brierley Hill Alliance	Lye Town	Whitwick Colliery
Bromsgrove Rovers	Nuneaton Borough	Wolverhampton Wanderers "A"
Brush Sports	Redditch	Worcester City Reserves
Burton Albion	Rugby Town	

Spencer made the best of starts to season 1955/56, winning their first six Birmingham League games. After beating Wolverhampton Wanderers "A" 3-0 at the Spencer Stadium on Saturday 17th September, Spencer were sitting proudly on top of the table. The next few weeks were though

Birmingham League First Division Table 1955/56 As at Saturday 17th September 1955 - Top 5							
	P	W	D	L	F	A	PTS
Banbury Spencer	6	6	0	0	17	4	12
Burton Albion	7	4	3	0	17	4	11
Lockheed Leamington	6	4	2	0	17	9	10
Brierley Hill Alliance	7	4	1	2	19	11	9
Nuneaton Borough	7	4	1	2	16	14	9

dominated by the FA Cup. Spencer may have lost 4-0 at home to Aylesbury United in the FA Cup four seasons previously but there was to be no slip up against the Delphian League amateurs this time as the Buckinghamshire side were beaten 7-0 at the Spencer Stadium in a First Qualifying Round game with Colin Whetton and Barry Thomas both getting hat-tricks. A healthy crowd of 2,980 had also turned out to watch the game.

The Second Qualifying Round brought Isthmian League Oxford City to the Spencer Stadium. The local derby, as with previous cup games between the sides, attracted a large crowd with 4,759 coming through the turnstiles to see a 3-1 win for the Gay Puritans, Spencer's goals coming from Tommy McGarrity, Jack Harrison and Barry Thomas. The Third Qualifying Round saw Spencer at home to another Isthmian League side, Wycombe Wanderers. Despite a goal from Harry Meadows, Wycombe won 2-1 but this was certainly no disgrace as the Wanderers went on to win the Isthmian League championship that season and therefore, by doing so, stake a fair claim to being the best amateur side in the country. Another impressive crowd, this time 3,479, turned up to see the game and, together with attendances in the earlier rounds of the competition, this gave a significant boost to finances.

Spencer's league results, after their exit from the FA Cup, through to the end of February 1956 were good enough to keep up their challenge for the Birmingham League Championship. February was particularly impressive with the club playing four league games and winning them all. At the end of that month Spencer were second in the table and looking as though they had every chance of taking the title. Though they were a point behind leaders Nuneaton Borough, they had a game in hand on the Warwickshire side.

However, March and April of 1956 were to be very disappointing for Spencer as they could only pick up eight points from their 10 league games and dropped out of the Championship race. Nevertheless, Spencer finished the season with 52 points from 38 games and this earned them a third place finish in the First Division of the

An impressively dressed Oxford City supporter entertains the Spencer Stadium crowd prior to the FA Cup game against Oxford City on Saturday 8th October 1955. FA Cup games against City in the 1950s attracted large crowds – this game saw 4,759 in attendance.

Birmingham League just four points behind champions Nuneaton Borough and one point behind runners-up Stourbridge.

The visit of Championship chasing Nuneaton Borough on Saturday 21st April attracted one of the biggest ever crowds to the Spencer Stadium for a league game, 4,541. Whilst this was an exceptional one-off attendance, the successful season had also resulted in a general increase in attendances compared to the previous year. Treasurer Eric Lowe reported at the club's AGM in July 1956 that attendances had increased by 50% from an average of 1,432 to 2,148. Despite the increase in gates, it was though only because of donations of £3,721, including from the "Britannia Club", that the football club managed to break-even.

Spencer's success during season 1955/56 had been built on a solid defence, having conceded only 40 league goals, the lowest by any club in either division of the Birmingham League that season. Secretary/manager Jimmy Cringan at the AGM reflecting on the season said "I felt we couldn't lose the

Birmingham League First Division Table 1955/56
As at Saturday 25th February 1956 - Top 7

	P	W	D	L	F	A	PTS
Nuneaton Borough	27	19	4	4	81	43	42
Banbury Spencer	26	19	3	4	56	21	41
Lockheed Leamington	27	15	4	8	68	43	34
Stourbridge	22	13	4	5	42	32	30
Rugby Town	28	11	8	9	63	61	30
Brush Sports	21	14	1	6	40	28	29
Bromsgrove Rovers	28	11	7	10	54	52	29

Birmingham League First Division Final Table 1955/56

	P	W	D	L	F	A	PTS
Nuneaton Borough	38	24	8	6	109	55	56
Stourbridge	38	24	5	9	85	48	53
Banbury Spencer	38	23	6	9	68	40	52
Lockheed Leamington	38	21	6	11	96	60	48
Burton Albion	38	20	7	11	82	48	47
Brierley Hill Alliance	38	18	8	12	91	81	44
Brush Sports	38	20	4	14	58	56	44
Bedworth Town	38	16	7	15	74	60	39
Wolves "A"	38	17	5	16	70	60	39
Bromsgrove Rovers	38	14	10	14	74	67	38
Halesowen Town	38	15	6	17	75	74	36
Walsall Reserves	38	13	9	16	66	68	35
Shrewsbury Town Res	38	13	7	18	84	87	33
Rugby Town	38	12	9	17	72	86	33
Worcester City Res	38	14	4	20	65	95	32
Whitwick Colliery	38	10	11	17	62	87	31
Bilston	38	10	8	20	53	100	28
Hinckley Athletic	38	12	3	23	75	83	27
Redditch	38	7	10	21	50	101	24
Lye Town	38	7	7	24	50	103	21

Championship, but we did. There was never a finer defensive play in this class of football right up until the time it cracked and we paid the penalty." Defenders, however, he continued were easy to get, it was forwards that were difficult and expensive, "but there are not going to be any stones unturned in strengthening this forward line." He was able to confirm that centre-forward Ray Powell who had experience in the Football League with Swansea City and Scunthorpe United and had been at Kettering Town for four seasons, being their top goalscorer for the last two, had signed to play for Spencer for season 1956/57.

CHAPTER 17

Seasons 1956/57 and 1957/58

The early months of season 1956/57 saw Spencer comfortably in the top half of the table without showing the sort of form which suggested that they might be serious title contenders. The FA Cup should have seen a relatively comfortable passage through the first couple of rounds. A 3-0 away win at Hellenic League Abingdon Town in the Preliminary Round was duly recorded but the First Qualifying Round saw an embarrassing 1-0 loss away to another Hellenic League side, Witney Town. The following week's Banbury Guardian described Spencer's loss as "their most humiliating post-war defeat" describing Witney Town as a "little amateur club… ..with a team of nearly all local lads" adding that the Hellenic League could hardly be rated on a par with the Warwickshire Combination in which Spencer's reserve team played but "here were Witney, beating Spencer's team of professionals, ten of whom have been with Football League clubs."

After the exit from the FA Cup, league results continued to keep Spencer well up in the top half of the table and after three consecutive wins towards the end of December the club were, as the new year dawned, in 6th place with 22 points from 17 games and with games in hand on the teams above them, there was still hope that a

Birmingham League Table 1956/57 As at Saturday 29th December 1956 - Top 7							
	P	W	D	L	F	A	PTS
Brierley Hill Alliance	23	14	2	7	44	36	30
Walsall	20	11	5	4	52	30	27
Aston Villa "A"	22	12	2	8	63	48	26
Burton Albion	18	10	4	4	52	37	24
Rugby Town	21	9	5	7	45	43	23
Banbury Spencer	17	10	2	5	38	24	22
Tamworth	18	7	7	4	42	38	21

continuation of the recent good run could put Spencer in contention right at the top of the table.

One notable game that did take place in the first half of season 1956/57 occurred on Saturday 22nd December 1956 when Spencer played their first ever competitive game under floodlights, a Birmingham League game at leaders Brierley Hill Alliance which Spencer won 1-0. The reporter from the Banbury Guardian was though not impressed with Brierley Hill's lights, writing "Spencer made a winning but farcical debut in competitive floodlit football at top of the table Brierley Hill Alliance. The whole floodlighting business was a needless extravagance that did not prove worthwhile. Neither the gate nor the game profited by the later kick-off and there were large areas of the pitch in virtual darkness." Spencer players complained afterwards that they had often lost sight of the ball in the air, and even of each other. Spencer manager Jimmy Cringan was also not pleased with the experiment, describing it as a waste of time when he saw the small crowd. "The only reason I agreed to it was because the Brierley Hill club assured me it would help them financially," he said, "That can hardly have been the case."

Spencer may have had reservations about Brierley Hill's lights but floodlighting was by this time here to stay and clubs up and down the country, even at non-league level, began to install lighting of sufficient standard to play competitive football though, as mentioned in an earlier chapter, floodlighting did not appear at the Spencer Stadium in the lifetime of Banbury Spencer Football Club.

Birmingham League First Division Final Table 1956/57							
	P	W	D	L	F	A	PTS
Walsall Reserves	38	23	8	7	95	48	54
Bromsgrove Rovers	38	22	7	9	93	61	51
Tamworth	38	20	9	9	94	62	49
Burton Albion	38	17	11	10	98	74	45
Rugby Town	38	19	7	12	80	68	45
Lockheed Leamington	38	16	10	12	84	65	42
Banbury Spencer	38	17	7	14	87	71	41
Aston Villa "A"	38	17	7	14	93	79	41
Bedworth Town	38	16	8	14	85	75	40
Brierley Hill Alliance	38	18	3	17	62	77	39
Wolves "A"	38	16	6	16	84	79	38
Atherstone Town	38	16	5	17	100	99	37
Worcester City Res	38	14	7	17	82	107	35
Nuneaton Borough	38	14	6	18	76	75	34
Stourbridge	38	13	8	17	66	68	34
Shrewsbury Town Res	38	13	7	18	74	90	33
Oswestry Town	38	12	8	18	71	86	32
Halesowen Town	38	10	9	19	74	96	29
Brush Sports	38	10	7	21	59	80	27
Whitwick Colliery	38	6	2	30	42	139	14

The second half of season 1956/57 began with Spencer losing three of their four league games in January, thus removing any lingering hopes of the club getting into the Championship race. Results from February onwards though were good enough for Spencer to comfortably finish in the top half of the table, 41 points from 38 games earning them 7th place.

With the club failing to mount a serious challenge for the Championship, crowds were disappointingly low throughout 1956/57. Despite the top half finish, the average attendance dropped by 44% to 1,212, the average for 1955/56 of 2,148 only being exceeded once in 1956/57. However, though gates had fallen dramatically, the club only lost £28 due to donations of £4,765 from the Supporters Club and the Britannia Club Pool. The club's reliance on these two organisations for their survival had become increasingly evident over recent seasons with over 70% of the club's income now coming from these sources rather than gate receipts.

Referring to the season at the club's AGM in July 1957, secretary/manager Jimmy Cringan commented "One of the most worrying seasons I have ever had in football. We had so many injuries that the team was completely upset. But I say quite honestly that we did well to finish as high up in the league with all these injuries." He went on to criticise high wages and said players were getting more and more expensive each year and more difficult to obtain. "Players are never worth the money they are getting" he declared "but you have got to pay it. You can pay them £15 a week and they are still no good."

At the AGM, Cringan was able to announce that he had signed two new wing men with Football League experience for the new season and had brought back

Dennis McQuillan

centre-forward Barry Thomas to the club. The wide men were right winger Ronnie Steel and left winger Dennis McQuillan.

Dennis started out as a junior with Derby County and progressed to make a total of 18 Football League appearances for them, scoring 1 goal, between seasons 1952/53 and 1955/56 inclusive. He then had short spells with Aldershot and then Luton Town the following season without making a first team league appearance for either club before he joined Banbury Spencer. He stayed at Spencer for just the one season and was a regular in the side making 38 first team appearances and scoring l1 goals. Dennis was very versatile in that he played in all of the forward positions during the season though he usually played either on the left wing or at centre-forward.

Ron Steel began his career with Bishop Auckland before joining Third Division North side Darlington in the summer of 1949. He made his Football League debut for the Quakers in the opening game of the 1949/50 season going on to make, over the course of three seasons, 66 league appearances for them. Ron later played for Headington United and Bedford Town before joining Banbury Spencer. He missed just one Birmingham League game in season 1957/58 and played in the first seven games of the following season but in early October 1958 he was dropped in favour of Stan Arthur and left the club the following month.

Spencer did not begin season 1957/58 well, picking up just three points from their first five league games. However, the club then had a four game winning league run from Tuesday 10th September through to, and including, Saturday 5th October. This saw Spencer climb up to fourth place just two points behind leaders Wolverhampton Wanderers "A" and raised hopes that the club could get into the Championship race.

Meanwhile, Spencer had exited the FA Cup at the first hurdle, though to be fair this was not unexpected as they were drawn away to Southern League high-flyers Headington United in the First Qualifying Round. Spencer put up a decent performance to only go down 1-0 and at least a share of the estimated gate of 5,000 was some consolation.

Spencer's league form during November and December of 1957 was exceptionally good, picking up 13 points out of a possible 16. A 3-0 away win at Stourbridge followed on Saturday 4th January 1958 and after this game Spencer had climbed up to second place in the table, just a point behind Wolverhampton Wanderers "A" and with a game in hand on the leaders.

Though Spencer lost a couple of games in January, the two they won kept them in touch

Birmingham League Table 1957/58 As at Saturday 5th October 1957 - Top 6							
	P	W	D	L	F	A	PTS
Wolves "A"	8	6	1	1	27	15	13
Hereford United Res	10	6	1	3	20	11	13
Bilston	7	6	0	1	22	8	12
Banbury Spencer	9	5	1	3	23	15	11
Walsall Reserves	8	5	1	2	18	15	11
Burton Albion	10	4	3	3	15	14	11

Birmingham League Table 1957/58 As at Saturday 4th January 1958 - Top 5							
	P	W	D	L	F	A	PTS
Wolves "A"	21	11	5	5	53	39	27
Banbury Spencer	20	12	2	6	44	23	26
Burton Albion	21	10	6	5	37	29	26
Brierley Hill Alliance	18	11	3	4	34	23	25
Walsall Reserves	21	11	3	7	41	38	25

with the leaders but any hopes of a challenge for the Championship were to be dashed in February of 1958 as they lost all four league games that month. It did not get much better in March either as only one point was collected from the four games played that month. At the end of March, Spencer had disappointingly dropped down to the bottom half of the table and were in 12th place with 29 points from 31 games. Spencer did finish the season well, collecting 11 points from their last seven games, which proved enough to see them climb up to finish the table in 9th place out of 20 clubs with 40 points from 38 games.

The club's financial position at the AGM in the summer of 1958 showed little change from the previous season. Average attendances for Birmingham League games had fallen from 1,200 to 1,033 and again it was only donations from the Britannia Club, this season totalling £4,775, which had enabled the club to continue, the loss for the year being thus restricted to £114.

The club also announced at the AGM that it had purchased the Spencer Stadium ground, which up to this point had been leased, from the estate of the late Oliver J Stockton. The purchase price of £2,000 was funded by a donation from the

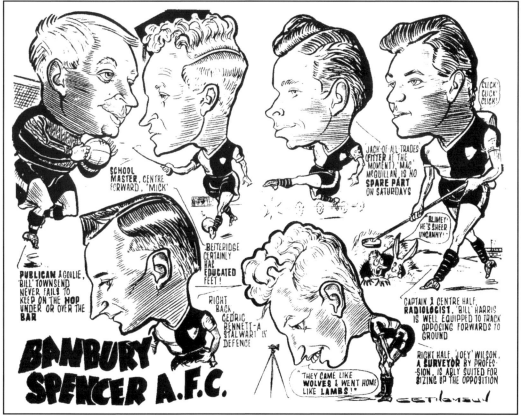

Banbury Spencer 1957/58

Caricatures of some of the Banbury Spencer players for season 1957/58. This appeared in the Banbury Advertiser on Wednesday 29th January 1958.

Supporters Club of £500, a donation from the Britannia Club of £1,000 and an interest free loan of £500 from Spencer (Banbury) Limited. Secretary/Manager Jimmy Cringan stressed that the ground was being bought by the football club and that there was no tie-up with Spencer (Banbury) Limited and commented "It is a fine thing to have one's own ground. Being able to purchase the Stadium means that the town will have a ground of its own for all times."

Birmingham League First Division Final Table 1957/58							
	P	W	D	L	F	A	PTS
Wolves "A"	38	24	6	8	116	64	54
Walsall Reserves	38	24	4	10	83	60	52
Brierley Hill Alliance	38	22	6	10	82	61	50
Bilston	38	21	1	16	85	65	43
Bromsgrove Rovers	38	19	5	14	85	65	43
Stourbridge	38	17	9	12	67	63	43
Lockheed Leamington	38	17	7	14	73	52	41
Shrewsbury Town Res	38	17	7	14	85	71	41
Banbury Spencer	38	18	4	16	76	63	40
Hereford United Res	38	15	8	15	63	59	38
Burton Albion	38	14	8	16	60	65	36
Tamworth	38	14	7	17	57	57	35
Nuneaton Borough	38	13	7	18	68	79	33
Hinckley Athletic	38	14	5	19	69	81	33
Bedworth Town	38	12	9	17	61	78	33
Aston Villa "A"	38	13	7	18	68	92	33
Worcester City Res	38	13	7	18	48	68	33
Rugby Town	38	12	8	18	50	70	32
Gresley Rovers	38	10	5	23	59	100	25
Atherstone Town	38	8	6	24	46	88	22

Notice placed in match officials changing rooms – from season 1956/57. This demonstrates the importance that the Banbury Spencer club placed on respect for the officials.

CHAPTER 18

Seasons 1958/59 and 1959/60

Season 1958/59 began with Spencer winning both their Birmingham League games in August, a 3-2 home win over Hinckley Athletic before Aston Villa "A" were beaten 4-0, also at the Spencer Stadium, with centre-forward Denis Packwood scoring hat-tricks in both games.

In the first week of September and for the second consecutive season, Spencer departed from the FA Cup at the first hurdle, this time going down 3-0 at home to Isthmian League amateurs Oxford City. Though the FA Cup was still a relatively attractive proposition for supporters with 2,790 going through the turnstiles, over two and a half times the club's first two home league attendances of the season, the 2,790 was nearly 2,000 less than the 4,759 who had watched the sides at the Spencer Stadium in the same competition just three seasons earlier.

After this disappointment, Spencer went on to pick up five points from their next five league games which, following on from their opening two wins, was enough to see them, after games played on Saturday 18th October 1958, in 6th place with 9 points from 7 games.

However, from Saturday 25th October through to Saturday 20th December, Spencer lost eight consecutive league games and after losing on the latter date 2-1 at home to Oswestry Town, the club had plummeted down the table to bottom place with just the nine points from 15 games played and in real danger of relegation to Division Two of the Birmingham League. Crowds had fallen to very low levels towards the end of this losing period. The opening two home league games of the season had seen crowds of just over 1,000 but this losing run took its toll on attendances with just 390 paying to come through the Spencer turnstiles for the Oswestry game.

A double over West Bromwich Albion "A" over the Christmas period did though put an end to the losing run and then much improved form throughout the second half of the season saw Spencer steadily climb up the table to finish comfortably in the top half,

Birmingham League First Division Table 1958/59 As at Saturday 20th December 1958 – Bottom 5							
	P	W	D	L	F	A	PTS
Hinckley Athletic	16	4	3	9	31	39	11
Aston Villa "A"	15	5	1	9	29	44	11
WBA "A"	15	4	2	9	33	35	10
Stourbridge	16	4	2	10	30	46	10
Banbury Spencer	15	3	3	9	23	34	9

Birmingham League First Division - Final Table 1958/59							
	P	W	D	L	F	A	PTS
Wolves "A"	34	26	7	1	91	40	59
Oswestry Town	34	22	4	8	96	58	48
Brierley Hill Alliance	34	20	4	10	85	50	44
Bromsgrove Rovers	34	15	10	9	62	56	40
Tamworth	34	15	8	11	51	58	38
Lockheed Leamington	34	15	7	12	85	59	37
Banbury Spencer	34	15	6	13	59	55	36
Walsall Reserves	34	15	4	15	66	68	34
Brush Sports	34	14	6	14	54	61	34
Bilston	34	12	7	15	57	66	31
Hereford United Res	34	11	9	14	53	74	31
Bedworth Town	34	12	6	16	55	56	30
Shrewsbury Town Res	34	11	7	16	54	54	29
WBA "A"	34	11	6	17	77	75	28
Stourbridge	34	11	3	20	67	90	25
Halesowen Town	34	10	5	19	79	112	25
Aston Villa "A"	34	9	6	19	63	86	24
Hinckley Athletic	34	7	5	22	55	91	19

their final total of 36 points from 34 games earning them 7th place out of 18 teams. Despite the results achieved in the second half of the season, attendances remained disappointing, the three home games in March, for example, all attracting gates of under 500.

At the club's AGM in August 1959 it was confirmed that the drop in attendances was from an average of 1,330 the previous season to 856 in 1958/59. Donations totalling £4,371 from the Supporters Club and Britannia Club had, as in recent years, saved the club from making a large loss. Such donations, due to falling gates, now accounting for over 75% of income.

Season 1959/60 followed a remarkably similar pattern to the previous season. Spencer's league campaign began well enough with five points from their first three games, a 4-3 home win over Walsall Reserves on opening day was followed by a 3-3 draw away to Birmingham City "A" and then an impressive 8-1 home win over Bedworth Town. Right winger Alan Cox scored four of Spencer's goals against Bedworth; oddly these were the only goals he scored in his one season with the club. The first three games had seen Spencer score 15 goals, Ron Eele netting 5, Alan Cox 4, Trevor Thomas 3, Terry O'Brien 2 and Johnny Hicks 1.

In the FA Cup Spencer got past Spartan League side Marlow 3-0 away in the First Qualifying Round but they found amateurs Oxford City too good for them in the Second Qualifying Round, as they had in the previous season at an earlier stage, this time losing 5-1 at the White House Ground.

Spencer's league form from Monday 7th September through to the end of November was very disappointing with the club picking up just three points from nine games. Despite the good return from their first three league games of the season, after a 1-1 draw at home to Bilston on Saturday 28th November, Spencer had just 8 points from 12 games and were one from bottom of the table.

Though there was a home victory over Tamworth at the beginning of December,

Birmingham League First Division Table 1959/60 As at Saturday 28th November 1959 – Bottom 5	P	W	D	L	F	A	PTS
Bedworth Town	13	5	2	6	18	31	12
Atherstone Town	12	5	1	6	20	23	11
Stourbridge	12	4	1	7	15	31	9
Banbury Spencer	12	3	2	7	26	24	8
Leicester City "A"	14	3	2	9	22	37	8

Birmingham League First Division Table 1959/60 As at Saturday 19th December 1959 – Bottom 5	P	W	D	L	F	A	PTS
Stourbridge	15	6	1	8	23	37	13
Leicester City "A"	17	5	2	10	32	40	12
Bedworth Town	14	5	2	7	18	33	12
Atherstone Town	14	5	1	8	24	30	11
Banbury Spencer	15	4	2	9	30	32	10

Birmingham League First Division - Final Table 1959/60	P	W	D	L	F	A	PTS
Bromsgrove Rovers	34	23	8	3	94	36	54
Birmingham City "A"	34	22	6	6	90	50	50
Wolves "A"	34	20	4	10	75	39	44
Bilston	34	17	6	11	82	77	40
Walsall Reserves	34	13	12	9	54	37	38
Brierley Hill Alliance	34	17	3	14	59	48	37
Leicester City "A"	34	15	6	13	75	70	36
Tamworth	34	15	4	15	55	52	34
Brush Sports	34	15	4	15	54	63	34
Atherstone Town	34	15	3	16	80	75	33
Lockheed Leamington	34	15	3	16	59	58	33
Hereford United Res	34	14	5	15	64	75	33
Halesowen Town	34	15	1	18	63	84	31
Banbury Spencer	34	10	7	17	60	71	27
WBA "A"	34	9	6	19	53	75	24
Stoke City "A"	34	7	8	19	48	76	22
Stourbridge	34	10	2	22	47	82	22
Bedworth Town	34	7	6	21	44	88	20

Spencer lost their other two games that month. As Spencer's last game in December was on Saturday 19th December, the club went into both Christmas and the New Year in bottom place in the table with just 10 points from 15 games. This was the second consecutive season that Spencer had at this point occupied a basement position.

As in the previous season, results were better in the second half of the season. Though Spencer's 17 points from 19 games was only mid-table form it was enough to pull them away from the bottom of the table and they finished in 14th place out of 18 teams with 27 points from 34 games. This was though the club's lowest finish to date since joining the Birmingham League for season 1954/55.

Though the league season was far from a success, there were four players who played in all 34 Birmingham League games. These were right back Alan Bury, left back Albert Ashcroft, inside left Tommy McGarrity and centre-forward/inside left Trevor Thomas. Joey Wilson, who had begun his career as a right winger with Spencer back in season 1946/47, missed just one Birmingham League game this season, playing now most games in the right half back position.

With very mediocre league form and an early exit from the FA Cup, the highlight of season 1959/60 was, without doubt, the club's second ever appearance in the final of the Birmingham Senior Cup. Spencer reached the final as follows:

Round 1	31 Aug	Away	Bedworth Town	W	2-1	Alan Rees, Johnny Hicks
Round 2	10 Oct	Home	Stourbridge	W	5-2	Ron Eele (2) (1 Pen), Trevor Thomas, Terry O'Brien (2)
Q-Final	07 Nov	Home	Cradley Heath	W	6-1	Johnny Hicks (3), Les Washington, Trevor Thomas, Terry O'Brien
S-Final	16 Jan	Away	Rugby Town	D	2-2	Trevor Thomas, Johnny Hicks
S-Final Rep	27 Feb	Home	Rugby Town	D	0-0	(after extra time)
S-Final Rep2	19 Mar	Home	Rugby Town	W	4-0	Tommy McGarrity (2), Bernard Brock, Trevor Thomas

The final was played on Saturday 2nd April 1960 at Leamington's Windmill Ground. As in Spencer's other Birmingham Senior Cup final appearance, eleven seasons previously, the opposition were Nuneaton Borough. Nuneaton were now a Southern League Premier Division side, so Spencer were very much the underdogs but they put up a decent performance, only losing 1-0. The winning goal came in the 57th minute and was rather fortunate as former Scottish International and Preston North End centre-forward Angus Morrison, then player/manager of Borough, missed his kick in front of goal with the ball hitting the front of his leg and rolling away into the far corner of the net leaving Spencer goalkeeper John Whitehouse helpless. Spencer even had two strong appeals for penalties later in the half but the referee on both occasions waved play on.

The Banbury Spencer line up for the final against Nuneaton Borough was: John Whitehouse, Alan Bury, Albert Ashcroft, Joey Wilson, Bill Harris, Alan Rees, Johnny Hicks, Terry O'Brien, Trevor Thomas, Tommy McGarrity, Bernard Brock.

With the club bottom of the table at Christmas for the second consecutive season, it is perhaps not surprising that spectator interest fell once more. At the club's poorly attended AGM in August 1960 it was reported that first team gates had dropped from an average of 856 in the 1958/59 campaign to just 526 for season 1959/60. Gate receipts from both first and reserve team games of £986 compared to club expenditure of £5,142. Donations from the Britannia Club Pool of £3,790 and other income had though helped to restrict the club's loss for the year to £216. The club's treasurer Eric Lowe described the club's financial position as "going downhill".

Programme Cover Season 1959/60.

Most supporters though were to find the comments made by secretary/manager Jimmy Cringan at the AGM to be of most interest. The Banbury Advertiser began their report of the meeting as follows "Will Jim Cringan, who is in his 25th season with Banbury Spencer Football Club, retire from his post as secretary-manager next year? After listening to his speech at the Banbury Spencer annual meeting, many of the 21 supporters present think this is quite likely." After attacking supporters for not being patient enough with young players, the press for the way that reporting now consisted almost entirely of a detailed analysis of weaknesses, in their opinion, of the team rather then a report of the events of the match and players generally for a lack of commitment, Cringan stated he was willing to resign if the club wanted to appoint a new manager. He said that his heart and soul was still with Spencer but "If the town, members, supporters and the committee wish to appoint another manager in my place there will be no ill-feeling or bickering from me." A further comment was made on the club's falling attendances, a major factor in his view was television, "When you watch a team like Real Madrid on television and then you go along to see local football, you realise it is little more than rubbish."

CHAPTER 19

Jimmy Cringan's Final Season

Prior to the start of season 1960/61, the Birmingham League had been re-structured. There had been suggestions for many years that what the Birmingham area needed was a league restricted to just first teams of football clubs. A meeting of the clubs took place on Thursday 10th March 1960 to discuss and then vote on this issue. However, a two thirds majority was required for the change and with so many reserve and "A" sides in the league this was not obtained. Banbury Spencer, and most of the other first team clubs, were very disappointed with this outcome and two weeks later at a special meeting, 14 clubs made the decision to resign from the Birmingham League and start their own league for the following season. These clubs were Atherstone Town, Banbury Spencer, Bilston, Brierley Hill Alliance, Bromsgrove Rovers, Cradley Heath, Darlaston, Dudley Town, Evesham United, Hednesford, Lockheed Leamington, Redditch, Stourbridge and Lye Town. Kidderminster Harriers, who had given notice that they were withdrawing from the Southern League at the end of the season, said they would welcome this development and also be willing to join.

Such a rebellion was, of course, a major concern to the Birmingham League and they then opted to try and form a league for just the first team clubs within the framework of the League with the reserve and "A" teams playing in their own division. This in turn upset the clubs with reserve and "A" sides in the League and as a result all the Football League reserve and "A" sides opted to resign and form their own "Midland Minor League". It was now no longer necessary for the "rebels" to form a new league and the reserve sides of the Southern League clubs, Hereford United, Wellington Town, Cheltenham Town and Worcester City who were left had no choice but to leave the Birmingham League and they all joined the welcoming Warwickshire Combination for season 1960/61.

Thus, for the first time since Banbury Spencer had moved into Birmingham based football back in season 1935/36, there were to be no reserve or "A" sides visiting the Spencer Stadium. The loss of these sides did though reduce the number of clubs in the Birmingham League down to just 22 and the

Birmingham League Final Table 1960/61							
	P	W	D	L	F	A	PTS
Bilston	42	33	5	4	149	51	71
Bromsgrove Rovers	42	30	7	5	140	48	67
Lockheed Leamington	42	29	4	9	125	46	62
Redditch	42	28	5	9	113	54	61
Brierley Hill Alliance	42	24	12	6	87	36	60
Kidderminster Harriers	42	23	7	12	99	58	53
Stourbridge	42	21	8	13	119	64	50
Atherstone Town	42	20	8	14	97	80	48
Tamworth	42	20	7	15	86	71	47
Banbury Spencer	42	21	5	16	108	92	47
Halesowen Town	42	20	6	16	106	90	46
Stratford Town	42	18	6	18	85	85	42
Sutton Town	42	19	1	22	88	82	39
Evesham United	42	16	3	23	76	89	35
Moor Green	42	14	6	22	76	99	34
Bedworth Town	42	14	5	23	78	96	33
Hednesford	42	13	5	24	73	123	31
Lye Town	42	11	7	24	65	112	29
Cradley Heath	42	8	9	25	73	143	25
Boldmere St. Michaels	42	7	5	30	49	118	19
Dudley Town	42	6	5	31	50	152	17
Darlaston	42	4	0	38	46	199	8

two division structure was therefore abandoned, with all member clubs forming one division. There were thus a number of clubs from Division 2 moved up to Division 1 which, at least in the short term, arguably reduced the standard. The full list of clubs in the Birmingham League for season 1960/61 was as follows:

Atherstone Town	Darlaston	Moor Green
Banbury Spencer	Dudley Town	Redditch
Bedworth Town	Evesham United	Stratford Town
Bilston	Halesowen Town	Stourbridge
Boldmere St Michaels	Hednesford	Sutton Town
Brierley Hill Alliance	Kidderminster Harriers	Tamworth
Bromsgrove Rovers	Lockheed Leamington	
Cradley Heath	Lye Town	

Spencer began their league campaign for season 1960/61 well enough, picking up eight points from their first six games. However, a first hurdle exit in the FA Cup on Saturday 10th September, losing 4-1 away to Hellenic League amateurs Abingdon Town, was another cup embarrassment for the club and the "hangover" from this defeat appeared to last the rest of the month as Spencer lost all their remaining three league games that month. Now around mid-table, this was a position that Spencer held until the end of the season, finishing in 10th place with 47 points from 42 games.

With the club not challenging for any honours, gates fell to a new low with the average attendance for the season being just 350. This was particularly disappointing considering the number of goals seen at the Spencer Stadium during the season, an average of five per league game. Spencer had few problems scoring goals, their 108 league goals being the highest number scored by the Club in a season in their history. Five players got into double figures, Harry Ironmonger and John Redding both scored 18, Johnny Hicks 16, Trevor Thomas 14 and Bill Harris 12. Spencer's problems were at the other end of the field where 92 were conceded.

The big news of the summer of 1961 was announced by the club on Tuesday 6th June. This was that after 25 years Jimmy Cringan was stepping down as the club's manager though he would be remaining as the club's Secretary. Cringan said he was pleased to have served the club "I have played in top-class football but I can honestly say that my happiest years have been in Banbury. The supporters here have been the best I have ever worked with." The new manager, announced at the same time as Cringan's departure, was to be Norman Rees who had been the club's Chief Scout for the previous four years.

Norman Rees was able to announce at the club's AGM,

Norman Rees

held at the end of July 1961, that he had signed local Aynho based youngster Pete Svenson. After leaving school, Pete had played for village side Souldern until signing for Oxford United at the age of 18. He had a year at Oxford, playing regularly for their reserve side before signing for Banbury Spencer upon his release. He already had Spencer club connections as his father Stan had played a game for the club in the Birmingham Combination in season 1945/46. Playing usually either at inside right or right half, he was a regular in the side for the remaining four years of the club's existence as Banbury Spencer, making a total of 149 first team appearances, scoring 30 goals. Pete also went on to play for Spencer's successor club Banbury United in the 1960s and 1970s making over 400 appearances for them.

Pete Svenson

Four weeks prior to the AGM, the new manager had announced that the club had signed for the following season one of the most experienced Football League players ever to appear for the club, centre half Roy Warhurst. Roy made 9 Football League appearances for Sheffield United between seasons 1946/47 and 1949/50 but it was after joining Birmingham City in March 1950 that he established himself in League football. Whilst at Birmingham he made a total of 213 Football League appearances and was club captain in season 1956/57. In the summer of 1957 he moved to Manchester City and later played for Crewe Alexandra and Oldham Athletic. After making a total of 330 Football League appearances in his football career he then left the full time game at the end of season 1960/61 to join Banbury.

Roy Warhurst

CHAPTER 20

Spencer at Gay Meadow in the FA Cup First Round

Season 1961/62 began with experienced summer signing Roy Warhurst installed as club captain. He led Spencer to victory in their first two Birmingham League games of the season, a 3-2 away win at Redditch on Saturday 19th August and then a 5-0 win at Dudley Town two days later. Spencer made it three league wins out of three on the second Saturday of the season when Hednesford were beaten 9-1 at the Spencer Stadium with Johnny Redding, Trevor Thomas and Kevin Cornwell all getting hat-tricks.

Spencer's first three league games in September were all away but their impressive start to the season continued, with them remaining unbeaten in those games, picking up five points out of six. After the last of those three games, a 2-1 win at Stratford Town on Saturday 16th September, Spencer had 11 points from six games played and were in

Birmingham League Table 1961/62 As at Saturday 16th September 1961 – Top 6						
	P	W	D	L	F	A	PTS
Lockheed Leamington	8	7	1	0	25	9	15
Banbury Spencer	6	5	1	0	24	7	11
Kidderminster Harriers	6	5	1	0	19	9	11
Bromsgrove Rovers	5	4	1	0	23	5	9
Brierley Hill Alliance	6	3	3	0	9	3	9
Moor Green	7	4	1	2	17	11	9

second place in the Birmingham League table with games in hand on leaders Lockheed Leamington.

Meanwhile, Spencer had got through their first FA Cup game of the season, winning 4-1 at Chesham United on Saturday 9th September in the First Qualifying Round with both Kevin Cornwell and Pete Svenson getting two goals each. The FA Cup then dominated the next eight weeks at the football club. A relatively comfortable 4-1 home win over Hellenic League side Abingdon Town in the Second Qualifying Round followed, Johnny Redding getting a hat-trick, before Spencer came up against old rivals Oxford City in the next round. Spencer had home advantage and this time beat the Isthmian Leaguers 3-1 with Redding getting all three goals. The attraction of the FA Cup and importance to generating interest within the town was again evident as 2,784 came through the Spencer turnstiles for the Oxford City game. The win over City set up a Fourth Qualifying home game against Southern League First Division side Yiewsley (a few years later they renamed themselves Hillingdon Borough) with a prize of a place in the First Round Proper and the possibility of a game against a Football League side to the winners.

Whilst Yiewsley were not in the top division of the Southern League, they were expected to provide stiff opposition and had as player/manager one of the most famous footballers ever to play competitively at the Spencer Stadium, Jackie Milburn. "Wor" Jackie was a footballing legend on Tyneside, being a local lad born in Ashington who went on to make over 350 Football League appearances for Newcastle United, scoring 177 league goals and playing a key part in them winning the FA Cup three times in five years in the early 1950s. He also made 13 appearances for England, scoring 10 goals.

Banbury Spencer v Yiewsley
Programme Cover.

However, on Saturday 21st October 1961, Milburn and the rest of his Yiewsley team were "blown away" in a seven minute spell early in the first half as Spencer raced into a 3-0 lead. Harry Ironmonger put Spencer in front in the 12th minute and just over a minute later it was 2-0 through Johnny Redding before five minutes later Kevin Cornwell scored the third. Yiewsley then piled on the pressure trying to get back into the game but the Spencer defence held firm and five minutes from half time Johnny Hicks finished all of the visitor's hopes with a fourth goal much to the delight of most of the 3,135 crowd. Spencer were able to ease off in the second half and with no further goals the 4-0 win took Banbury Spencer into the First Round Proper of the FA Cup for just the second time in their history.

How Spencer Reached the FA Cup First Round Proper

Round		Opposition	Result	Spencer Goalscorers
First Qualifying	A	Chesham United	W 4-1	Kevin Cornwell (2), Pete Svenson (2)
Second Qualifying	H	Abingdon Town	W 4-1	Trevor Thomas, Johnny Redding (3)
Third Qualifying	H	Oxford City	W 3-1	Johnny Redding (3)
Fourth Qualifying	H	Yiewsley	W 4-0	Harry Ironmonger, Johnny Redding, Kevin Cornwell, Johnny Hicks

Spencer were not rewarded with a home game in the First Round Proper. However, unlike the previous occasion that they had reached this stage back in season 1947/48, when they were drawn against then Southern League side Colchester United, this time they were to meet a Football League side, being drawn away at Gay Meadow to mid-table Third Division Shrewsbury Town, the game to be played on Saturday 4th November 1961.

To get their supporters to the game, the Spencer Committee stated that, provided at least 400 people were willing to travel, they would arrange for a "Special Train" to run from Banbury to Shrewsbury. With FA Cup fever gripping the town it was evident within 24 hours that there was indeed sufficient demand.

Members of the Football Club committee, together with volunteer supporters, were in the railway sidings on the morning of the game to decorate the front of the engine ready for the journey with a headboard proclaiming "Banbury Spencer - Gay Puritans to Gay Meadow".

The reserved coach for players and officials was though rather empty when it left Banbury for there was only one local player in the side, that being Pete Svenson. With most of the others living around Birmingham, there was a mass pick-up of players, and Birmingham based manager Norman Rees, at Snow Hill.

With many more supporters travelling by coach and private car it was estimated by the local press that there were around 1,000 Spencer supporters amongst the crowd of 7,750.

Spencer's opening spell was good enough to raise optimism amongst the Spencer supporters who had

---

F.A. CUP (1st ROUND PROPER)

Banbury Spencer v. Shrewsbury Town

SATURDAY, NOVEMBER 4th, 1961

Provided 400 Supporters wish to travel to Shrewsbury on Saturday, November 4th, accommodation on a Special Train can be arranged at a

Fare of 16/- (Children 8/-)

The Train will leave Banbury at approximately 11 a.m.

Fill in your name and address below and hand in together with the appropriate fare(s) to any Committee Member of the Football Club or Supporters' Club, or at Lynott's Hairdressing Salon in Bridge Street before Saturday evening next, October 28th. You may hand in your Booking at the Stadium on Saturday. Stand tickets for the Shrewsbury game will be on sale at the Stadium on Saturday. Prices as follows : 6/6, 5/6, 5/-.

Name ....

Address ....

Fare (if for more than one please indicate) ....

The "Gay Puritans to Gay Meadow headboard on the front of the engine.

travelled to encourage them. However, Jimmy McLaughlin, Shrewsbury's Northern Ireland international left winger, had different ideas and in the 17th minute he put the home side ahead. Cutting in from the left he beat Bob Williams in the Spencer goal with a low drive into the bottom corner. The Shrewsbury half-backs took command after this and their forwards swept downfield repeatedly with Spencer having to be content with sporadic breakaways. The Spencer defence did though hold out until the half hour mark when right winger Mike Kenning slammed home a loose ball from ten yards to put Shrewsbury 2-0 up.

The second half was all Shrewsbury. Dave Dann and Pete Svenson got through a lot of hard work and Roy Warhurst never seemed prepared to admit defeat but nothing could hold Shrewsbury now. Their half backs completely dominated the midfield play and were even coming up into attack. The experienced Arthur Rowley was the inspiration behind Shrewsbury's third goal after 61 minutes. He sent Kenning away on the right and McLaughlin put the finishing touch to the right winger's centre with a rocket header. A spell of continuous pressure on the Spencer defence followed and after 69 minutes Kenning got Shrewsbury's fourth. Rowley then added number five after 80 minutes with a well taken goal that gave Williams no chance.

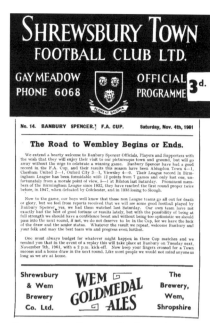

The around 1,000 Banbury fans were then a minute later finally given something to cheer about when John Redding thrust his way down the middle and beat the advancing goalkeeper Mike Gibson from the edge of the penalty area with a hard drive. Spencer took heart from this and Redding was given another chance moments later

Shrewsbury Town v Banbury Spencer Programme cover.

but the Shrewsbury defence gave him no time to pick his spot and he could do no better than prod the ball into the goalkeeper's hands. This was Spencer's last effort. Shrewsbury were though still not finished and with the Banbury backs visibly tiring under the onslaught of the superbly fit Shrewsbury professionals they added two more goals. Malcolm Starkey scored the sixth and Rowley added a final flourish by netting the seventh a minute from time to make the final score 7-1.

Despite the hammering, local and national press recognised Spencer's fighting spirit and, though outclassed, how they had never given up and were always trying to play good football. Newspaper headlines included "Gallant Spencer Swamped", "Shrewsbury's experience was too much for gallant Spencer", Furthermore Spencer were badly disadvantaged when inside-left Kevin Cornwell was concussed in a collision with the Shrewsbury goalkeeper 15 minutes before half time. Though he played on, until very near the end when he left the field completely, the injury undoubtedly reduced his effective-

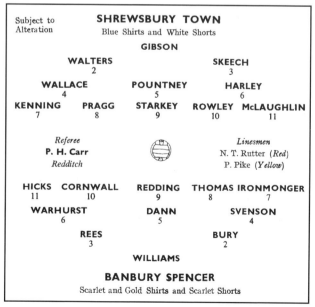

ness and threw the whole attack out of gear. Banbury had not though been disgraced in defeat and richly deserved the sympathetic applause of the 7,750 spectators as they trooped off. Manager Norman Rees said "They were too good for us. They were faster to the man and to the ball. That's what full time training does for a team." But Rees was not disheartened "There will always be a next time in the FA Cup. We were not disgraced."

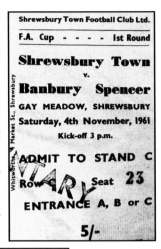

Shrewsbury Town Football Club Ltd.

F.A. Cup - - - - 1st Round

Shrewsbury Town

v.

Banbury Spencer

GAY MEADOW, SHREWSBURY

Saturday, 4th November, 1961

Kick-off 3 p.m.

ADMIT TO STAND C

Row   Seat 23

ENTRANCE A, B or C

5/-

The Banbury Spencer team at Shrewsbury was: Bob Williams, Alan Bury, Alan Rees, Pete Svenson, Dave Dann, Roy Warhurst, Harry Ironmonger, Trevor Thomas, John Redding, Kevin Cornwell, and Johnny Hicks.

Visitor's Page BANBURY SPENCER

Pen Pictures

Bob Williams (Goal). Engineer. Lives at Oldbury and played for Stourbridge before linking up with Banbury last season. Was signed on professional forms a fortnight ago.

Alan Bury (Right Back). Draughtsman. Comes from Coventry and has been with Banbury for six seasons now. Has had plenty of experience in Birmingham League football.

Alan Rees (Left Back). Petrol pump maintenance engineer. Son of manager Norman Rees, Alan was born in Wales but has lived in Birmingham since he was seven. Previously had spells with Blues and Kidderminster.

Peter Svenson (Right Half). Electrician. Lives just outside Banbury and played for Oxford United last season, moving to the Spencer during the summer.

Dave Dann (Centre Half). Car factory worker. Was an amateur goalkeeper with Birmingham, but has now settled down at centre-half with Banbury. Now a professional.

Roy Warhurst (Left Half). Scrap metal merchant. The former Birmingham skipper is well known in the Midlands. After leaving St. Andrew's he had spells with Manchester City, Crewe, and Oldham before joining Banbury this summer.

Harry Ironmonger (Outside Right). Factory worker. Was an amateur with Villa and then Northampton. Signed for Banbury when he was demobbed two years ago.

Trevor Thomas (Inside Right). Bricklayer. Played as an amateur with Birmingham before moving to Banbury. Comes from Tyseley, and was originally a centre-forward.

Johnny Redding (Centre Forward). Factory worker. A former Youth International left back, Redding was on Wolves' books for some time. Signed for Banbury 18 months ago, and is now a professional.

Kevin Cornwall (Inside Left). Accountant. Lives in St. Andrew's Road, Small Heath, and was an amateur with Blues. Now several League clubs would like to sign him.

John Hicks (Outside Left). Shopkeeper. Was with Coventry City, has been a regular in the Banbury forward line for several seasons now.

The Banbury Spencer player profiles which appeared in the programme.

Spencer supporters at Gay Meadow.

Below is a photo of the Spencer team that played against Shrewsbury Town. Spencer's five games in the 1961/62 season's FA Cup had seen them use just 12 players. Except for the Third Qualifying Round game against Oxford City, when Alan Morton replaced Johnny Hicks on the left wing, the side was the same throughout the campaign. The photo below was actually taken at the Spencer Stadium prior to the Second Qualifying Round home game against Abingdon Town.

Back Row (Left to Right): Jack Ballinger (Trainer), Alan Bury, Pete Svenson, Dave Dann, Bob Williams, Roy Warhurst, Alan Rees, Unknown (ordinary clothes). Front Row: (Left to Right): Harry Ironmonger, Trevor Thomas, John Redding, Norman Rees (manager), Kevin Cornwell, Johnny Hicks.

The "Special Train" en route to Shrewsbury – photo by Keith Pirt.

Due to their FA Cup and also Birmingham Senior Cup commitments, Spencer, between playing away to Sutton Town on 4th September 1961 and at Halesowen Town on 18th November 1961, managed just three Birmingham League games. Not surprisingly therefore, Spencer had slipped right down the table from their second place back in mid-September to a mid-table position in mid-November. After games played on Saturday 11th November, though Spencer had an impressive return of 12 points from 8 games, they were only in 11th place out of the 21 teams, albeit with at least four games in hand on all of the clubs above them.

There were high hopes that Spencer would continue their good league form

Birmingham League Final Table 1961/62							
	P	W	D	L	F	A	PTS
Lockheed Leamington	40	31	5	4	124	37	67
Brierley Hill Alliance	40	27	8	5	96	37	62
Bromsgrove Rovers	40	27	5	8	117	56	59
Bilston	40	24	6	10	135	62	54
Kidderminster Harriers	40	24	6	10	102	58	54
Tamworth	40	21	7	12	91	63	49
Redditch	40	21	7	12	89	67	49
Sutton Town	40	21	7	12	104	79	49
Halesowen Town	40	21	6	13	97	75	48
Banbury Spencer	40	18	8	14	107	84	44
Stourbridge	40	18	6	16	84	70	42
Stratford Town	40	17	7	16	82	73	41
Darlaston	40	14	7	19	70	93	35
Moor Green	40	13	8	19	67	79	34
Atherstone Town	40	12	9	19	70	97	33
Bedworth Town	40	11	6	23	61	86	28
Lye Town	40	10	6	24	45	89	26
Evesham United	40	8	5	27	74	132	21
Boldmere St. Michaels	40	9	3	28	59	126	21
Hednesford	40	6	4	30	58	155	16
Dudley Town	40	3	2	35	45	159	8

that they had shown earlier in the season and soon be climbing up the table. This failed to happen though, with the club losing four consecutive league games from mid-December to mid-January which kept them firmly entrenched in mid-table territory, a position they held right through to the end of the season, finishing with 44 points from 40 games and in 10th place.

Leading league goalscorers this season were Johnny Redding with 35 goals, Trevor Thomas 20 and Kevin Cornwell 14. Inside left Kevin Cornwell's tally was obtained from just 21 games as he was transferred to then Fourth Division Football League side Oxford United in early March for a fee of £500.

Kevin Cornwell was born in Birmingham and spent time as a youngster with Birmingham City. However, after being released, his football career drifted into Sunday League matches in the Birmingham area. Eventu-

Kevin Cornwell admiring the travelling case presented to him, in recognition of his services to the Spencer club, at an end of season dinner watched by players John Perrin (left) and Johnny Redding (right). By this time Kevin was an Oxford United professional having joined them from Spencer at the beginning of March 1962.

ally he was spotted by Norman Rees, Banbury Spencer's then Chief Scout and he brought him to the Spencer Stadium.

Kevin made his debut for the reserve team against Saltisford Rovers (the former name of the current Racing Club Warwick club) in a Warwickshire Combination game at the Spencer Stadium on Saturday April 2nd 1960 scoring two goals in a 3-2 win. His first team debut came right at the end of that season on Monday 25th April in a Birmingham League game away to West Bromwich Albion "A". However, he did not play in the first team the following season until as late as the 21st January 1961, that game saw Kevin score a hat-trick at Bromsgrove Rovers but despite this, and a goal from Spencer's Harry Ironmonger, the home side won the game by the remarkable score of 10 goals to 4!! He went on to score another 6 goals for the club in the remainder of that season.

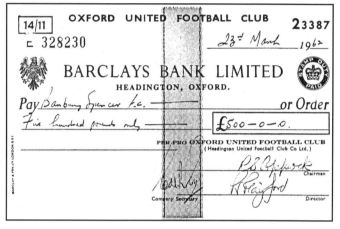

The summer of 1961/62 saw the man who had brought Kevin to the Spencer Stadium, Norman Rees, installed as manager of the club and his signing showed some outstanding form, scoring 18 first team goals up to and including Saturday 3rd March 1962. He certainly impressed Oxford United in an Oxfordshire Professional Cup game at the Manor Ground on Wednesday 28th February 1962 because they immediately opened negotiations to sign him. This transfer was completed the following week for a fee of £500 which was stated in the press to be a then record fee paid by Oxford United for a non-league player. Ironically the manager of Oxford United at the time, Arthur Turner, had been manager of Birmingham City whilst Kevin was at St. Andrews as a youngster! After making 26 Football League appearances and scoring 10 goals for Oxford United between March 1962 and April 1964 he was given a free transfer at the end of season 1963/64. Kevin then played for Cambridge United and Cheltenham Town before joining Nuneaton Borough in the summer of 1965 but just a few weeks into the 1965/66 season he agreed to return to the Spencer Stadium to play for Spencer's successor club Banbury United.

The club's AGM in August 1962 was very positive. John Gilkes, the club's Treasurer, reported the financial position as "considerably better than last year, with the club completely out of debt." Though home support had dropped off after the exit from the FA Cup at Shrewsbury, gate receipts for the season were £1,669, double the year before which were £827, albeit the gate receipts for the season were again dwarfed by contributions from the Britannia Club and Supporters Club of over £4,000.

1960s crowd at the Spencer Stadium.

In addition, the £500 fee for the sale of Kevin Cornwell had been a bonus and finances had been sufficiently good enough to enable the club to repay, in December 1961, the loan of £500 it had received from Spencer (Banbury) Limited to help them buy the Spencer ground back in 1958.

Manager Norman Rees stated at the AGM that he thought it had been a satisfactory season commenting "We were doing well at the start of the season but didn't have the reserve strength to keep us there." He then told the meeting that the club would, in future, be making more effort to find local talent which could be brought through to the first team and that former Spencer left winger Bob Kinder had agreed to re-join the club to scout for promising youngsters in the Banbury area.

With the Spencer Works having had less involvement in the affairs of the football club in recent years it was also confirmed at the AGM that the administration had now been moved out of Spencer House to 36 High Street, Banbury to which all future correspondence was to be addressed. These premises were already in use as the offices for the Britannia Club and Supporters Club. It was stated that this move was in recognition that the Football Club was, in effect, no longer a works team.

There were many who had scoffed at the signing by Spencer of Roy Warhurst in the summer of 1961. They doubted his ability to stand up to a full season of Birmingham League fixtures, having only managed eight League games for Oldham Athletic the previous season and they reckoned, with him also having to travel from his Cheshire home, he wouldn't play in half the club's matches. The doubters were though proved to be wrong as Roy missed just one first team game all season and

A second view of a 1960s crowd at the Spencer Stadium.

that was due to him being badly delayed on the roads by fog. An unnamed club official in a local paper was quoted as follows "Roy has proved one of the best club men we have ever had. We only wish we had a few more like him."

Banbury Spencer F. C.
Spencer House, Britannia Road,
Banbury, Oxon.

Telephone:-
Office 2265
Ground 3354

Dear Sir:

You are selected to play V .... Redditch ....

at Banbury .... on Saturday 6th October, 1962 ....

Transport leaves .... at ....

Kick off ......3......... p.m.

Meeting Report at Stadium 2.15 p.m.

Yours truly,

J. A. Cringan

Banbury Spencer Supporters Badge showing the Banbury Cross and the lady on a white horse. A design similar to the badge worn on the club shirts, see chapter 12.

In the days before texts, emails and even widespread home telephones, this was the way that the club used to inform players that they were selected for matches – the posting of selection cards. This card is signed by Jimmy Cringan, who at this time was no longer manager but still with the club as Secretary.

CHAPTER 21

Seasons 1962/63 and 1963/64

The first two games of season 1962/63 appeared to justify the general optimism shown at the August AGM. The Birmingham League had been renamed the West Midlands League for the start of the season and Spencer began their campaign with a 6-0 away win at Boldmere St Michaels, followed by a 5-0 home success over Darlaston with centre-forward Johnny Redding getting hat-tricks in both games. A crowd of 670 had seen the Darlaston game and despite Spencer losing their next two league games, the local football public again demonstrated the attraction of the FA Cup with the club's home First Qualifying Round game against Oxford City attracting a much higher attendance of 1,743. Spencer's run to the First Round Proper the previous season had generated much early season interest but there was to be no repeat this time around as Spencer lost 2-0 to City, a big disappointment after the heroics of the previous season.

Spencer did respond positively to the FA Cup set-back by picking up nine points from their next five league games and after games played on Saturday 20th October 1962 were in third place in the table with 13 points from 9 games. This form was though not maintained and Spencer soon began to struggle to stay in touch with the top sides. Nevertheless,

West Midlands Regional League Table 1962/63 As at Saturday 20th October 1962 – Top 6							
	P	W	D	L	F	A	PTS
Lockheed Leamington	11	9	2	0	31	8	20
Stourbridge	9	7	1	1	26	7	15
Banbury Spencer	9	6	1	2	27	10	13
Bromsgrove Rovers	9	5	3	1	26	16	13
Brierley Hill Alliance	10	5	3	2	22	18	13
Halesowen Town	10	5	2	3	27	16	12

a 6-0 home win over Boldmere St Michaels on the Saturday before Christmas followed by a fine 1-0 home win over runaway league leaders Lockheed Leamington on Boxing Day took Spencer up to fifth position just three points behind second placed Stourbridge. However, the season was then seriously disrupted by one of the severest winters that the country had experienced for many years. The snow and icy conditions meant Spencer, after beating Lockheed Leamington on Boxing Day, did not play again until a home game against Moor Green on Saturday 9th March.

Though the game against Moor Green was won 4-3, the remainder of the season was very disappointing with only three more league wins in 18 games and Spencer slipped down to the bottom half of the table finishing in 13th place out of 20 clubs with 34 points from 38 games. What was also of concern was the financial implications of the decline in attendances over the course of the season. The first few league games had attracted an average of around 650 through the Spencer Stadium turnstiles but by early December crowds had declined to such an extent that only 220 and 278 saw the first two home games that month and even the attractive Boxing Day derby against Lockheed Leamington only attracted 357. And with Spencer showing such poor form when football resumed after the lengthy spell of bad weather, there was no significant upturn in attendances later in the season.

Season 1962/63 was Roy Warhurst's second and final season with Banbury Spencer. He had played in 22 out of the first 23 West Midlands League games of the season but was then troubled with a knee injury, managing just two out of the club's final 15 league games, and it was no surprise that he was not retained by the club at the end of the season.

May 1963 saw Jimmy Cringan retire after 27 years service to the club. He had started with Spencer as player/manager in 1936. He finished playing in 1940 but after the War had ended he then combined the manager's job with that of secretary. After stepping down

West Midland Regional League Final Table 1962/63							
	P	W	D	L	F	A	PTS
Lockheed Leamington	38	28	7	3	119	40	63
Stourbridge	38	26	6	6	98	38	58
Hednesford	38	22	7	9	97	62	51
Halesowen Town	38	23	3	12	97	53	49
Atherstone Town	38	23	3	12	95	57	49
Kidderminster Harriers	38	20	8	10	88	53	48
Bromsgrove Rovers	38	21	5	12	95	52	47
Brierley Hill Alliance	38	17	10	11	70	62	44
Dudley Town	38	19	6	13	72	71	44
Stratford Town	38	15	12	11	52	48	42
Tamworth	38	15	8	15	69	69	38
Darlaston	38	15	4	19	80	71	34
Banbury Spencer	38	15	4	19	86	86	34
Bilston	38	14	6	18	78	95	34
Moor Green	38	11	9	18	59	95	31
Lye Town	38	11	5	22	56	99	27
Bedworth Town	38	9	4	25	61	88	22
Redditch	38	6	9	23	44	95	21
Boldmere St. Michaels	38	4	5	29	39	133	13
Sutton Town	38	4	3	31	45	133	11

from the manager's post in 1961, he then spent a final two years with the club as secretary. Laurie Hicks, who had been Assistant Secretary, was appointed to the Secretary's position. With Cringan's departure, Hicks was now the only remaining football club committee member who worked at Spencer, though Robert Allen, albeit having no involvement in the day to day running of the club, remained its President.

A football club committee meeting on 21st May 1963 discussed the possibility of the club dropping "Spencer" from its name and being renamed "Banbury Football Club". The committee's view was that, due to the club's now independence from the Spencer Works, this was desirable provided club President and founder Robert Allen was in agreement. This story was picked up by the local press with the Banbury Advertiser on Wednesday 29th May 1963, under the headline "Goodbye Spencer – Hello Banbury!", stating that "Banbury Spencer is no more. In future it will be known as plain Banbury". This proved to be premature though, as the President replied to a letter from club Chairman Robert Bradshaw, the letter requesting his views on the dropping of "Spencer" from the club's name, that he deplored the idea of a change of name but added that if it were to be altered perhaps "Banbury Cross" or "Banbury Cavaliers" may be appropriate. At a subsequent committee meeting on 16th July 1963 it was then

Banbury Spencer Programme Cover Season 1962/63.

agreed that the club's name for season 1963/64 should remain as "Banbury Spencer".

There was a major development at the club's committee meeting on June 4th 1963. Manager Norman Rees, who was on the committee, was asked to leave the room so that the rest of the committee could discuss the possibility of appointing a player/manager to save costs. The committee, after discussion, agreed that this option was desirable and that they should advertise the position in both the Birmingham Mail and Birmingham Sports Argus. Rees was called back to the meeting and informed that he would be offered the position of Scout for the club, a position he had held when working under Jimmy Cringan. Rees left the meeting stating that he would consider the offer but later informed the committee that he wished to sever all connections with the club. The parting of the ways was not amicable, with Rees speaking to the Banbury Advertiser stating "When the announcement was made to me last Tuesday, it came as a complete bombshell." In a bitter attack on the committee, Rees accused them of trying to humiliate him by offering him his former job of Scout "I wouldn't consider this for one minute" he said "I have had to take the can for the penny pinching methods of the club. I shall leave Banbury without regrets." Rees had been Spencer manager for two seasons, being in charge for the club's run to the First Round Proper of the FA Cup the previous season and had subsequently moved to Banbury from Birmingham to take up the tenancy of the Angel public house. He stated he would be looking to give up the tenancy and get back into football elsewhere adding "I have had a raw deal from the club and the sooner I can get away, the happier I shall be."

On Tuesday 16th July 1963 the club announced that Keith Volpe (pronounced Volpay), aged just 27, was to be the new player/manager of the club. Volpe had originally been on Manchester City's books joining them in 1953 initially playing at centre-forward though he was by the time he came to Spencer playing at centre-half. He never made the first team at City and in 1956 began playing for his home-town club Hereford United, firstly as an amateur then as a professional. After several seasons at Edgar Street he decided he was not progressing and moved on to Newport County, again without making a first team appearance, and then Merthyr Tydfil staying for two years at Penydarren Park.

Volpe's tenure as Spencer's player/manager began with the club being unbeaten in their first four league games of the season, albeit three of those were drawn. The season's FA Cup campaign began with a relatively easy 4-0 home victory over Spartan League side Huntley & Palmers from Reading, the Spencer goals coming from Barry Holbutt (2), Graham Perkins and player/manager Keith Volpe. However, despite two goals from Perkins, Spencer then disappointed their supporters by going out in the Second Qualifying Round 3-2 at home to Athenian League amateur side Maidenhead United.

After losing to Maidenhead, Spencer returned to league action and though picking up just one win in their next four games, losing the other three, an excellent run of form in November, when the club won all four of their league games, gave Spencer at the end of that month a healthy total of 15 points from 12 games. However, due to having played a couple of games less than most of the other teams this was only good enough for 9th place out of the 19 teams. The run of success in November had been achieved without player/manager Keith Volpe in the side. He had, in fact, not played for the club since Saturday 12th October, Brian Stone having now established himself as the preferred choice at centre half.

West Midlands Regional League Table 1963/64 As at Sat 30th Nov 1963 – Top 10					
	P	W	D	L	PTS
Dudley	16	7	6	3	20
Stourbridge	15	9	2	4	20
Brierley Hill Alliance	16	8	3	5	19
Atherstone Town	14	7	4	3	18
Bilston	13	7	3	3	17
Tamworth	11	8	1	2	17
Bromsgrove Rovers	14	7	2	5	16
Hednesford	14	6	4	4	16
Banbury Spencer	12	6	3	3	15
Halesowen Town	10	7	0	3	14

Clearly the football club committee were expecting a player/manager to be good enough to play, with him not doing so the financial arguments for employing someone in that role that had been put forward the previous summer were not being realised. With him not playing, his influence and involvement in the club's affairs was also diminishing and he was asked to attend a committee meeting on 17th December 1963 in which a discussion on the player/manager position took place. The outcome of the meeting was that by mutual agreement Volpe left the club. Oddly he remained under contract with Spencer as a player and actually turned out for the reserve side later in the season.

Following the unsuccessful experimentation with a younger player/manager, the club reverted to a more traditional management choice and on Tuesday 4th February 1964 appointed Tom McGarrity as manager. Tom had started his playing career with Greenock Morton in Scotland before moving South of the Border to join Southampton though he only made five league appearances (in season 1952/53) for the Saints, He then had a spell with Heading-ton United (later to become Oxford United) making 13 Southern League ap-pearances for them, all in season 1953/54, prior to joining Banbury Spencer for season 1954/55, the first of seven seasons in which he was a regular in the Spencer first team. In his first five seasons at Spencer he played predominantly at inside right but in the final two years in which he was a regular he often played at wing half. He was still at Banbury at the time of his appointment to the manager's job, turning out for the Reserve team.

West Midland Regional League - Final Table 1963/64							
	P	W	D	L	F	A	PTS
Tamworth	36	29	2	5	88	35	60
Kidderminster Harriers	36	24	3	9	108	45	51
Halesowen Town	36	22	5	9	105	52	49
Bromsgrove Rovers	36	19	9	8	94	55	47
Dudley Town	36	19	7	10	90	63	45
Stourbridge	36	18	7	11	76	61	43
Hednesford	36	18	7	11	77	63	43
Bilston	36	14	11	11	70	60	39
Banbury Spencer	36	16	6	14	65	69	38
Atherstone Town	36	12	12	12	73	67	36
Brierley Hill Alliance	36	14	8	14	47	49	36
Lower Gornal Athletic	36	12	10	14	60	69	34
Lye Town	36	12	7	17	60	71	31
Darlaston	36	12	7	17	67	84	31
Stratford Town	36	11	7	18	48	78	29
Redditch	36	10	7	19	44	75	27
Moor Green	36	7	7	22	44	90	21
Bedworth Town	36	3	8	25	36	106	14
Sutton Town	36	2	6	28	41	101	10

Spencer's form in the second half of the season was that of a mid-table side and they duly finished 9th out of 19 clubs with 38 points from 36 games. The AGM in August 1964 was primarily concerned with the club's financial situation caused by falling support. Though the club had only made a loss of £200 on the season, this was due to the club drawing on reserve funds of the Britannia Club which had been built up over many years and were now fast being depleted. Attendances for West Midlands League games had averaged only around 400. Chairman of the club, Harry Price said "We have a lot of good people working for the club, but we lack support. It is a pity there is so much apathy in the town – this is shown in the very poor attendance at this meeting." The Banbury Advertiser reporting on the meeting used the following headlines "Does Banbury deserve Spencer FC?" and "Lack of support slated at Club and Supporters AGM".

The two photographs show Spencer players training at the Spencer Stadium around 1964. They give an excellent view of the old covered enclosure along the side of the ground. In both of them one can see Fabian Duru who was the first black player to play for the club. Fabian signed for Spencer in the summer of 1963 and was a Nigerian international having played for his country in the late 1950s and early 60s. He had just moved to Banbury from Liverpool to work for Switchgear, his stay in the UK being financed by the Nigerian Electricity Corporation. Whilst in the North West he had played for New Brighton and Prescott Cables. Fabian went on to make a total of 31 first team appearances for the club over the course of seasons 1963/64 and 1964/65.

CHAPTER 22

The Final Season

It was rather a mediocre start to season 1964/65 for Banbury Spencer, with the club picking up five points from their first six league games. An exit from the FA Cup at the first hurdle away to Oxford City, losing 2-1 at the beginning of September, had also done nothing to stimulate interest and excitement amongst supporters. Three consecutive league wins from Saturday 26th September, including a 7-2 home win over Halesowen Town and a 6-0 away win at Moor Green, did briefly raise hopes but they were short-lived and by the beginning of December the club were down into a mid-table position. Gates were now at an all time low and of major concern; the attendance for the home game against Redditch on Saturday 5th December was reported to be barely 250.

It was events off the field which were beginning to shape the future of semi-professional football in Banbury. Mid-September of 1964 saw the resignation of the club Treasurer John Gilkes who had held the position for four years. In explaining his departure he stated that he could see only a pessimistic future for the club as there was now a very poor following in the way of support and the Britannia Club Pool, now facing severe competition from similar schemes in the local area, was unable to provide the level of funds to finance the Spencer Football Club that they had done over many years. The minutes of a subsequent club meeting at the end of November 1964 confirmed that, at the present rate of use, all reserve funds held by the Britannia Club would be exhausted before the end of the season.

Events on the field then took a turn for the worse. Spencer lost seven consecutive league games from Saturday 12th December 1964 through to Saturday 6th February 1965 (inclusive) and had slipped down to 15th place out of 20 clubs with 16 points from 21 games. Gate receipts for the home games in February against Moor Green and Sutton Coldfield Town were just £14 and £12 respectively, under a third of what they had been for the first two home games of the season.

Saturday 23rd January 1965 had seen the death, from a sudden heart attack, of Club President and founder Robert Allen. Perhaps this was the final obstacle to the dropping of Spencer from the club's name as just over two weeks later at a committee meeting on Wednesday 10th February, it was agreed that from the start of the following season the name of the club would be changed from Banbury Spencer to Banbury United, subject to approval of the Football Association. The intended change was reported in the local press at the beginning of March, the article confirming that

West Midlands Regional League Table 1964/65
As at Saturday 6th February 1965
Bottom 7

	P	W	D	L	PTS
Lye Town	25	8	2	15	18
Banbury Spencer	21	7	2	12	16
Darlaston	22	5	6	11	16
Sutton Coldfield Town	23	4	6	13	14
Moor Green	19	4	2	13	10
Bedworth Town	23	4	1	18	9
Atherstone Town	21	2	1	18	5

a name change had been rumoured for some time but that most supporters were rather surprised at the choice of United as "Banbury Town" had been expected. The name change was subsequently formally approved by the Football Association at a meeting on 30th April 1965.

With Britannia Club reserve funds being rapidly diminished and no alternative sources of sufficient finance looking to be available as a replacement, January of 1965 saw the club giving serious consideration to withdrawing from the West Midlands League and operating on a purely amateur basis at a lower level. The minutes of a football club meeting on 28th January 1965 recorded that notification of withdrawal would have to be made by the 31st March 1965 to avoid a fine of up to £500.

However, February 1965 saw club officials approached by a group of local businessmen, led by Cyril Kyme, informing them that they would be interested in taking over the football club. With negotiations proceeding satisfactorily the club decided at the end of that month to continue in membership of the West Midlands League for the following season. Banbury Spencer's results from mid-February through to Tuesday 6th April did show some improvement with the club picking up nine points from eight games which did at least, albeit temporarily, halt the rapid slide down the table.

The group of local businessmen interested in taking over the football club proposed to form a company "Banbury United Football Club Limited" to which all the assets of the Banbury Spencer Football Club would be transferred. This was approved by the Banbury Spencer club at a committee meeting on 5th April 1965. The assets transferred included the freehold of the ground, the trustees of the ground giving it their full support. The story of the takeover finally hit the local press in mid April of 1965. The Banbury Advertiser on Wednesday 14th April carried a front page article under the headline of "Take over of Banbury Spencer F.C." The article included a statement from Banbury Spencer Football Club, of which the following is an extract:

"The Trustees and Committee of Banbury Spencer Football Club met Mr. C.A. Kyme and other interested parties on Monday April 5th 1965, for a discussion on the future of the club. As a result of those discussions, Mr Kyme and other local businessmen are to promote a new company Banbury United Football Club Limited to take over the existing assets and management of the club. It is hoped that members of the general public in Banbury who wish to keep a high standard of football in Banbury will be eager to subscribe for shares in the new company, to ensure that it has a very solid financial foundation...........The present Trustees and Committee of the Club have given their blessing to this new venture but all present at the meeting realised that it will only succeed if the sporting public of Banbury wish it and will it to succeed."

The Advertiser added its own comments to the club statement "Undoubtedly this move will prove a life saver for professional football in Banbury. In its present form the club, despite the enthusi-astic work of the committee, is dying on its feet. Playing results have gone from bad to worse. Finances have dwindled alarmingly and the support on the terraces has dropped right away. In fact, Banbury Spencer are now one of the poor relations of the West Midlands League - having to save money by taking the players to away matches in private cars. Yet the spirit amongst the players is excellent and it has not been for want of trying that Banbury are down with the "rats and mice" of the League. Now Banbury stand on the threshold of a new era. Shares will be offered to the public so that the fans will have a personal stake in the club if they so wish. And when all the shouting is over it will be the sporting public of Banbury that will eventually dictate whether the new club sinks or swims. The success of a club is measured by the number of people that pass through the turnstiles. Businessmen can give it a good start but it is the public that must keep it afloat."

Banbury Spencer's final game took place on Friday 30th April 1965, a home West Midlands League fixture against Brierley Hill Alliance. Spencer's line up was Dave McArthur, Evans, Mick Kennard, Pete Svenson, Jimmy Smith, Brian Stone, Doug Prosser, Barry Jones, Warwick Floyd, Bobbie Wickett and Norman Thomas.

Spencer went into the game having lost their previous eight league matches, scoring just 3 goals and conceding 26. For the whole of the first half it looked as though this losing sequence might be broken as Spencer looked the better side, going in front three minutes before the interval when left winger Norman Thomas ran onto a Warwick Floyd pass before slotting the ball past the goalkeeper. However, poor defending from Spencer enabled Brierley Hill to draw level 45 seconds after the interval and then just after the hour mark slack marking gifted the visitors a second goal.

Towards the end of the game the slow hand clap was heard around the ground and the smallest crowd of the season started to drift away long before the final whistle. The loss to Brierley Hill had extended the losing sequence to nine games. All of this was a sad way for Banbury Spencer Football Club to end their existence.

West Midland Regional League Final Table 1964/65

	P	W	D	L	F	A	PTS
Kidderminster Harriers	38	30	6	2	124	37	66
Halesowen Town	38	26	4	8	107	52	56
Dudley Town	38	27	1	10	103	42	55
Lower Gornal Athletic	38	23	6	9	74	50	52
Tamworth	38	24	4	10	101	69	52
Brierley Hill Alliance	38	23	4	11	87	58	50
Stourbridge	38	18	10	10	81	56	46
Bromsgrove Rovers	38	19	8	11	76	60	46
Walsall Reserves	38	21	4	13	75	61	46
Bilston	38	18	4	16	75	67	40
Hednesford	38	16	6	16	75	61	38
Redditch	38	13	8	17	55	56	34
Stratford Town	38	10	9	19	68	80	29
Lye Town	38	11	4	23	64	104	26
Banbury Spencer	38	11	3	24	79	99	25
Darlaston	38	8	9	21	69	112	25
Atherstone Town	38	8	4	26	59	121	20
Bedworth Town	38	8	3	27	39	95	19
Moor Green	38	7	4	27	44	108	18
Sutton Town	38	4	9	25	53	120	17